In their sympathetic and insightf Phillips helpfully point out that when a sensitive Christian soul realizes that a consumerist, politicized, fundamentalist, scandal-ridden Christianity looks nothing like the enduring beauty of Christ, deconstruction *is* conversion. Deconstruction doesn't have to be the end of faith; instead, it can be the beginning of a better faith. *Invisible Jesus* is a timely gift from a scholar and a pastor who genuinely want to help people find an expression of Christianity centered on Jesus Christ.

BRIAN ZAHND, author of *When Everything's on Fire*

Invisible Jesus takes a deep dive into what it means for people to wrestle with their faith and come out on the other side. Instead of shaming deconstructors for going through their own "dark night of the soul," Scot McKnight and Tommy Phillips argue that this reevaluation is a natural part of the faith process. This book can serve as a balm for those who are struggling to make sense of religion and for those who are worried by the number of people who seem to be leaving the church behind.

RYAN BURGE, author of *The Nones: Where They Came From, Who They Are, and Where They Are Going*

Scot McKnight and Tommy Preson Phillips rightly and deftly point out that those undergoing deconstruction are gifts to the church, not enemies, contrary to what some churches and pastors would have us believe. The problem is not those deconstructing; it is the American church that has collectively become something Jesus would find almost unrecognizable. This book is a call to repentance, a call for the American church to repent and follow Jesus instead of the idols of its own making. It is those deconstructing, among other canaries in the coal mine, who are calling the church to follow Jesus. May we listen closely; our salvation depends on it.

DR. MARLENA GRAVES, author and assistant professor of spiritual formation at Northeastern Seminary

Doubt, the dark night of the soul, and deconstruction—Scot McKnight and Tommy Phillips are no strangers to these experiences, for they have been through them as well. They point out, however, that despite what is wrong with the churches, church history, or contemporary Christianity, the best thing about it is still Jesus, and it is Jesus who calls us to himself. To whom else can we go? The pursuit of power, the lust for pleasure, and the drowning of our pain in the numbness of our devices don't work. McKnight and Phillips elegantly remind us that Jesus invites us to take his yoke upon ourselves, for he is good and gentle, and he offers us rest from our travails.

REV. DR. MICHAEL F. BIRD (PHD, University of Queensland),
deputy principal, Ridley College, Melbourne, Australia

It is truly difficult to recommend books for people who are walking through the deconstruction journey. Too many, sadly, belittle the experiences of people who are questioning their faith or the church. And too many seek to add fuel to the fire and almost seem to require the abandonment of Christian faithfulness. The message of *Invisible Jesus* is different. It offers a safe path forward for individuals who seek to love God and do so through the valley of their questions. For it is only in walking through those questions that the true life will be found.

A. J. SWOBODA (PHD, University of Birmingham) is associate professor of Bible and theology at Bushnell University and author of *The Gift of Thorns*

Deconstruction has become en vogue among a certain sect of Christians. That being so, other believers have responded to the rise of deconstruction with everything from questions to outright opposition. For some, deconstruction is a lifeline; for others, it is a ligature. Scot McKnight and Tommy Person Phillips give the church handles for seasoning this conversation with hope and a love that is Jesus-centered. If you, or someone you know, are asking questions about the Jesus of the Gospels, or have questions about the people who have questions, this is the book for you.

SEAN PALMER, author, *Speaking by the Number*,
and teaching pastor, Ecclesia Houston

I'm going to be a spoiler and give away the ending here: "If we must be disruptive, let's do it for Christ's sake." Disillusionment and deconstruction are disruptive. Are we willing to face what those who are leaving the church are seeing and saying, and then ask with Scot McKnight and Tommy Phillips, "What place will Jesus have in the church"? We need disruption. It is a tool the Spirit of God uses to help us face reality and lead us to beautiful repentance—to laying down our own illusions and waiting for resurrection in wonder. Let's embrace the disruption of the "invisible Jesus" as an invitation to collaborate with Christ in opening the door to the kingdom of heaven.

AIMEE BYRD, author of *The Hope in Our Scars* and
Recovering from Biblical Manhood and Womanhood

The local church plays an essential role in the lives of Christ followers for healthy growth and for their mission. *Invisible Jesus* raises some uncomfortable but valuable questions about whether we are contributing to the reasons some leave the church or are helping them stay and flourish in the church. We will read that the answers are not changing any historical core Christian beliefs, but they may lead us to change our thinking about how to live out these truths for the sake of future generations and the church.

DAN KIMBALL, vice president at Western Seminary and
author of *They Like Jesus but Not the Church*

The American church cannot afford to dismiss the issues Scot McKnight and Tommy Phillips address. They provide guidance for the church to become less bound by rules and more Jesus-centered, to listen and learn from those who are deconstructing, and to have a more Jesus-formed, Spirit-shaped faith. This book is a must-read for everyone who wants to knock down walls erected by culture or tradition and recover Jesus as the way, the truth, and the life for themselves and for the church.

JOYCE KOO DALRYMPLE, executive director of Refuge for Strength
women's ministry and author of *Women of the New Testament*

As I walk through the neighborhood around our church, I see beautiful houses being torn down and rebuilt every month. This visual image of deconstruction (or demolition) and reconstruction has been helpful as I think about the many people in my church who are rethinking their commitments, values, and beliefs regarding the life of Jesus and his church. *Invisible Jesus* gives pastors and church leaders a guide for navigating the current cultural moment in which so many are evaluating everything about their faith. There are very few people I trust more than Scot McKnight and Tommy Phillips to have a serious and practical intellectual conversation about the complexities and promises of faith. *Invisible Jesus* is a great resource for those who have done demolition but are still at work on the rebuild.

JOSHUA GRAVES, lead minister, Otter Creek
Church, and author of *The Simple Secret*

INVISIBLE
JESUS

INVISIBLE
JESUS

A BOOK ABOUT
LEAVING THE CHURCH
AND LOOKING
FOR CHRIST

Scot McKnight and
Tommy Preson Phillips

ZONDERVAN
REFLECTIVE

ZONDERVAN REFLECTIVE

Invisible Jesus
Copyright © 2024 by Scot McKnight and Thomas Preson Phillips

Published in Grand Rapids, Michigan, by Zondervan. Zondervan is a registered trademark
of The Zondervan Corporation, L.L.C., a wholly owned subsidiary of HarperCollins
Christian Publishing, Inc.

Requests for information should be addressed to customercare@harpercollins.com.

Zondervan titles may be purchased in bulk for educational, business, fundraising, or sales
promotional use. For information, please email SpecialMarkets@Zondervan.com.

ISBN 978-0-310-16233-9 (audio)

Library of Congress Cataloging-in-Publication Data

Names: McKnight, Scot, author. | Phillips, Thomas Preson, 1980- author.
Title: Invisible Jesus : a book about leaving the church and looking for Christ / Scot
    McKnight and Tommy Preson Phillips.
Description: Grand Rapids, Michigan : Zondervan Reflective, [2024]
Identifiers: LCCN 2024012438 (print) | LCCN 2024012439 (ebook) | ISBN
    9780310162315 (softcover) | ISBN 9780310162322 (ebook)
Subjects: LCSH: Belief and doubt—Religious aspects—Christianity. | Skepticism. | Church
    attendance. | BISAC: RELIGION / Christian Living / Social Issues | RELIGION /
    Agnosticism
Classification: LCC BT774 .M333 2024 (print) | LCC BT774 (ebook) | DDC 211/.8—dc23/
    eng/20240520
LC record available at https://lccn.loc.gov/2024012438
LC ebook record available at https://lccn.loc.gov/2024012439

Cover design: Jonlin Creative
Interior design: Denise Froehlich

Printed in the United States of America

24 25 26 27 28 LBC 5 4 3 2 1

To Watermark Church in Tampa, Florida

Contents

1 Encountering Jesus in Fundamentalism

Deconstruction is a rising trend in most American evangelical churches. Deconstructors themselves are sidelined, silenced, and sabotaged. For the most part, pastors and churches have been treating deconstruction as a symptom of a lack of information, a lack of discipleship, or rebellion against God. Perhaps we are looking at something new in Christianity—an upheaval that cannot be solved by a sermon series or even by a book cowritten by a Bible scholar and a pastor.

We believe something bigger is happening in the church, something that will continue to grow and that we dare not ignore. We believe deconstruction is a prophetic movement resisting a distorted gospel. It is not a problem; it is a voice. And we need to listen to what it is saying to the church.

At the heart of the rise of deconstruction is a loss of trust and confidence in the clergy. A significant Gallup Poll measuring the shift among people's trust in clergy concluded that in 1983, 64 percent of people trusted them. Two years later, in 1985, that number *grew* to 67 percent. But by 1990, it had dipped to 55 percent and by 1993 to 53 percent. We have seen no rebound from the 1990s to the present day. In 2009, the number dropped to 50 percent, hitting 36 percent by 2021. Today, approximately one in three persons in America trusts a clergyperson.[1] This roughly parallels the level of confidence people have in the institutional church, though the church rates a bit lower than clergy today at a dismal 31 percent. By comparison, in 1975, the percent of people who had confidence in the church stood at 68 percent.[2]

We also believe this new wave of deconstruction is not, as many religious leaders have suggested, something born of evil that must be denounced. We believe the work of deconstruction is often born of the Spirit, a movement of God attempting to bring the church back to Jesus. It is for Christ's sake that people today are walking away from churches. Stories of deconstruction challenge us because they are the exit interview many church leaders never have with those who leave the church. They never have them because they don't take the time to ask. We did:

ⓢ Shane — Aug 30

IMO, most people leave faith and/or the church because all of the raw beauty was drained from the story of Jesus by people with an agenda.

Our concern in this book is not with those wrapped up in the process of deconstructing their faith. We believe God is with them and for them in that process. Instead, we are concerned with those sitting in the pews next to them—how pew sitters treat those who doubt and how they respond to those who pose disruptive questions and raise subjects that church leaders do not want to talk about. Many of those labeled deconstructors are truth seekers who have identified abusive postures and beliefs but are now ostracized and treated as outsiders. They have had their voices unjustly silenced because those in the seats of power have dismissed their discernments, insights, and pressure points.

It's time for us to listen, to sit down, quiet our minds, and hear what those who are leaving "religion" are saying. In many cases, they were not given a chance to speak. Until now. And we can only report some of their concerns.

I (Tommy) have been a pastor for many years and live in Florida. The number of blog posts and social media posts sharing questions or stories of deconstruction that are forwarded to me by another worried, offended, or downright angry parishioner are almost as numerous as the sand on the beaches near me. Often the parishioner is pointing out a perceived error in that person, and they want me to set that person straight. And while I understand the concern about spiritual safety and the desire to make sure others stay on the right path, we have written this book to offer some wisdom, to help calm anxieties, and to encourage people to set aside the fears that arise when someone else's faith journey takes a path different from their own.

We also want to address those who have been through or are currently walking through the "dark night of the soul" of deconstruction. We hope you find a reassuring voice in this book, as we will not treat you with criticism and disdain. You are not the problem in your church. Well, maybe you are. But what if you are a good problem for the church? We believe people like you can be the canary in the coal mine, the unexpected, quiet voice through whom God is speaking.

We have nothing but encouragement for you. You have been placed in a difficult position—speaking truth to power and confronting the people who raised you in the faith. They may not like what you have to say, and you may need to oppose their teachings directly and respectfully. We acknowledge that yours is a lonely and painful path to walk, and our goal is to give everyone, both deconstructors and critics, the space to imagine a new way forward, a new vision of God's people that is beneficial, wise, loving, inclusive, healing, merciful, and, above all, Christlike.

Deconstruction is not new. Many at some point in their lives deconstructed the faith they grew up with. Some found a faith that survived that process; some haven't. In some cases, the survivors exit the Christian pond on the other side and create what one religion journalist called a "reorganized religion."[3] We'll have more to say about that later, but for now we'd like to point out that recent studies show that those who enter the dark tunnel of deconstruction most likely will *not* leave the faith and become a "None" or a "Done."[4] Press release: instead, they find another pocket of the Christian faith that fits what they believe, or they figure out how to form one that fits what they believe.

Both of us writing this book have gone through phases of deconstruction and have come out on the other side holding on to Jesus. But our stories are not the same. Scot's journey of deconstruction, back in the 1970s and '80s, is not the same as Tommy's. Tommy's predated postmodernism's deeper questioning of all truth. Still, there are many similarities.

Scot's Deconstruction Story

I (Scot) grew up in American fundamentalism. My parents were devout people. My mom read the *Our Daily Bread* devotional every morning with her black leather Scofield Bible open, and my father read his black leather Scofield Bible along with a commentary on the particular Bible book he was reading. When my father died in his ninetieth year, my mother gave me his Bible, which she called his "filing cabinet." I wasn't sure what she meant, but I quickly learned. Holding up his Bible, little notes and pictures fell to the floor like confetti. My father's Bible held all sorts of spiritual thoughts, notes, outlines, and newspaper clippings, tucked away for future reference. Growing up, we were at church every time its doors were open. Truth be told, we were there *before* they opened. We arrived early, before anyone else, because my mother had a key. We opened the doors for everyone else. Of course, that meant we were also the last to leave.

My parents were good people, to be sure. But there was a dark side to the fundamentalism they embraced, one feature of which stands out to me today—the pervasive vibe that no other church in our city was truly Christian. Certainly, there may have been an odd believer or two in a Methodist, Presbyterian, or Episcopalian church, but not among the numerous Roman Catholic churches in our area.

Lots of people in those churches smoked and drank, and most of their churches hosted junior high dances to usher in the weekend. These were all clear signs those people were not genuine Christians. As teens, we heard the lighthearted jab at our fundamentalism: "Why don't Baptists have sex before marriage?"

Answer: "Because they're afraid it will lead to dancing and drinking." I'll admit I inherited this suspicion. I'm sad to admit it, but I was suspicious of almost everyone. I believed very few people would go to heaven. Fortunately, we were among those who would.

This was largely true until I went to college—a fundamentalist school, mind you—and began to read more widely. And read I did. I knew from my freshman year I wanted to be a Bible professor so I began reading books to get myself ready. During college I read a lot of books by Bob Gundry and George Eldon Ladd that convinced me of the (very close to liberal) posttribulation view of the rapture (I later shifted from that view).

During my college years, I married my wife, Kris, and became a mediocre (at best) youth pastor at a small fundamentalist Baptist church. Then we moved to Chicagoland, and I went to seminary. By the time I was a year or two into seminary, I knew two things: *I knew what I no longer believed*, which was most of what I had grown up believing. The second thing I knew was something that scared me: *I knew I didn't know what I really did believe.* I knew this because a friend of mine was concerned about me and asked me what I believed so I wrote out an outline and gave it to him. He said to me, "This tells me what you don't believe. What *do* you believe?" It was a good question—one I wasn't ready to answer at that time. I was searching.

What is most noticeable to me now is that I did most of this deconstruction and reconstruction in silence. I had questions that would have led my mentors and friends to think I was going off the rails and abandoning the faith. Kris and I shared this journey together. I was the theologian so I was doing the probing. Kris was the listener who had her own questions, some of them fiercer than my own. I wasn't always capable to face the questions she asked, but we were in it together.

This was a time in American Christianity when love for Jesus was the fuel on the dry wood of society and church. It was the era of the hippie generation and the Jesus movement that started in California. Many Christians turned their backs on much of American fundamentalism to create a fresh version of faith with a more Jesus-shaped and Spirit-empowered church life.

My generation turned our backs on the American Dream, questioned the Vietnam War, and thought we could reform and revive the church with radical Bible study, spirited singing, and cool stickers on our Bibles. We attended prayer groups, Bible studies, and house groups where we were convinced we were all in, on fire, and sold-out for Jesus. We stayed away from pot and "got high" on Jesus, or, to fetch a newer expression, Jesus was dope. We wanted to change church music from organs and choirs to guitars and drums and singers with long hair who looked more like the Beatles than the Beach Boys. Larry Norman's "Why should the devil have all the good music?" became our mantra.[5]

We knew, or thought (depending on the level of our humility), that we had experienced God in ways deeper than our parents had and that we were going to change the world. As the old folk song put it, "Those were the days, my friend, we thought they'd never end."[6] But they did, or at least they did for me and my story. At one point, we got wrapped up in rapture speculation, wondering if we should even bother going to college (one of our friends didn't), and many of us considered forming a commune-like lifestyle. You already know—Kris and I went to college, thank God.

During this time, my deconstruction was already happening, and it continued through my pursuit of a PhD at Nottingham

University and into my early days as a professor. And alongside my deconstruction, I began to reconstruct what I believed; I deconstructed the faith of my upbringing and reconstructed the Christian faith. I've written this book with my friend Tommy because I want to share some of my journey with you. To be honest, I don't think my deconstruction has ever really ended.

I was a deconstructor and a reconstructor. I was reforming, reshaping, and reorganizing my faith. And I did this because the faith I grew up with no longer made sense—or at least enough sense to make it the foundation of my life. That was five decades ago, and had I not gone through that deconstruction phase, I would not have the faith I have today. I'm grateful for those who knew about my journey and left me alone—not entirely alone, but alone enough to find my way on the basis of what made sense to me. My deconstruction phase led me to find Jesus, who pointed the way in the reconstruction phase. On Jesus I reconstructed my faith.

I'm not alone in this experience. Many of those whose stories we tell in this book trace a similar journey. This is how Todd Hunter describes the experience, noting the importance of those people who didn't reject him:

> I have real empathy for those who are deconstructing elements of their faith. Such areas of spiritual life can, once on the other side of them, lead to constructive growth. The progress of a pilgrim is always the goal of my spiritual life. I have pursued this progress by staying on the path marked by the person and work of Jesus. I have survived by constantly making my way back to Jesus, to the nature of his being, his words, and his works.[7]

This is Tommy's story as well.

Tommy's Deconstruction Story

I (Tommy) grew up in Anaheim, California, until the age of twelve, when we moved to Tampa, Florida, where I still live and serve as a pastor. My father was involved in missions, and we spent many Sundays traveling to different churches, helping them establish youth ministries. Later, my father served as the director of an evangelical youth camp and a Bible institute. I grew up immersed in the Bible and evangelical church culture. After high school, I attended a very conservative two-year Bible college and then transferred to Liberty University, where I received two things: my BA in Religion, and a heavy load of doubt about Christianity, Jesus, and the church.

I returned home and immediately joined the steady stream of postgraduation Liberty students who were funneled into a new movement called Emergent Church, a collection of cohorts who gathered regularly outside of the church to ask the questions that were eating us up inside, questions hitched to traditional answers that made our faith untenable.

I can still pinpoint the exact second when I realized what I believed no longer made any sense. It was the moment my deconstruction began. I was at my doctor's office, and though I don't remember why I was there, I remember thumbing through a *National Geographic* sitting on an end table. I read an article about meteor strikes and how they have created holes so big they become massive lakes and mountain ranges. Some of these meteors have created explosions the equivalent of ten billion WWII-era atomic bombs, destructive enough to wipe out all forms of life for thousands of miles.

At the time I was barely holding on to a belief system that mandated the world had only been in existence for somewhere between six and eight thousand years. I held that view because

I believed holding it was necessary to hold on to Jesus. The two went together. I had been told that if I let go of one (the age of the earth), the other would go along with it (Jesus). I remember sitting in that office and feeling the weight of it all sink in, thinking, *Had humans been on this earth during these events, there would have been something about it somewhere in ancient history, at least in the Bible.* I muttered to myself, *Where is the record of this in the text?*

The evidence for the meteor hits was obvious and observable. But the evidence for my brand of Christianity, despite having consumed all of Lee Strobel's books, was becoming less and less convincing with every article I read, every museum I visited, and every moment I spent reading the book of Genesis. Every Sunday school volunteer and youth pastor had taught me that the earth was less than ten thousand years old. What was I supposed to do with that? How do you carry on when you believe something to be true that no one else in your life believes? It's terrifying.

I spent the next month thinking about meteors. Whenever someone mentioned Genesis, I thought *meteor.* Just a few years earlier, my youth pastor encouraged students in our group to boldly proclaim the gospel by pushing back against their science teachers. *Meteor.* I thought back to a class trip to a museum where the Christian school teacher stood at the exhibits and blocked the signage displaying the approximate year each dinosaur lived. *Meteor.* I felt like someone was hiding something. Someone, somewhere, was lying to me, and everyone else was covering it up.

I began to look at Christian leaders through squinted eyes. I had read things I could not unread. I had heard things I could not unhear, no matter how much I wanted to. The seeds of deconstruction had been planted and were beginning to take root. Eventually, those roots spread to every other part of my faith.

2 Hearing from Jesus in Our Doubts

I (Tommy) once had a conversation with a friend who was building a tiny house. Being a natural skeptic, I asked him if he thought this approach was really a better way to live. I had doubts that cramming all of your possessions into a three-hundred-square-foot house on the back of a fifth wheel and moving from place to place as a seminomad was actually enjoyable. He replied, "No, it's not, but this isn't about living *better*; this is a prophetic movement. Wages haven't budged in decades while the cost of living has skyrocketed unabated." Then he said something I remember to this day: "The tiny house is both a warning and a lifeline for those of us who are falling behind!" Ten years later, with chronic homelessness up 3 percent and disabled homelessness up 16 percent since 2020,[1] I have come to agree with his assessment of the movement. And I have come to view other movements as prophetic voices.

Like deconstruction.

It's Not What They Say It Is

The philosophy of deconstruction came to the forefront of intellectual discussions through a French thinker, Jacques Derrida, who sought to dismantle claims to truth, reality, and power. Indeed, by the time he was done, he all but maintained that all claims to truth are nothing but claims to power. Deconstruction is a method of dismantling power, which, in many cases, needs dismantling. And some people in the church today are doing that kind of deconstruction—an intellectual sorting out of Christian claims as claims to power. But there's another form of deconstruction at work among many evangelical Christians. It touches on power but dismantles it, not so much by assaulting power claims as by knocking truth claims off their perch.

The term *deconstruction* is on the rise across all social media platforms, and the number of articles about deconstruction has doubled in the last twelve months. A 2022 HarperCollins study found that one in four adults "have changed their spiritual or religious beliefs in the last couple of years."[2] No doubt, the COVID-19 era accelerated shifts and changes in how we view the world around us, and it apparently gave many Christians space to rethink the faith traditions they were raised in. Religion News Service reported that the pandemic was a period when 46 percent of young Americans began new forms of religious or spiritual practices.[3] Yet notice this interesting fact as described by RNS: the pandemic *strengthened* personal faith across the board. The social distance created by the pandemic seemed to have given people of faith an opportunity to walk away from a faith community they outgrew with minimal discomfort or confrontation.

And in most cases they were walking away to *another form of the Christian faith*. Most of those surveyed described their shift in belief as a "re-evaluation" or a "reconstructing," and about one in ten use the term *deconstruction*.

Again, an overwhelming number of those who deconstruct their faith don't walk away from the faith altogether but instead find another form of the Christian faith that fits them better. Olivia Jackson, author of *(Un)Certain*, quotes a UK church minister named George as saying, "The people who are done with church are not done because they lost their faith. They're done because the Church is done with faith."[4]

"A More Beautiful Way to Belong"

ROHADI NAGASSAR

Ironically, encountering barriers to belonging is a revelation of sorts that would otherwise go unnoticed. Previously disguised features in a world specifically built to marginalize select bodies become known as we encounter them. When we name these hidden pieces, the systems, the cultures, and the beliefs that seek to make us less whole, we begin to tear down the dividing wall. Naming divisions, questioning old ways, and embarking on new paths also has a name: deconstruction. In this way, deconstruction is a pathway unto liberation from all that ain't right in the world. It's a process of finding a more beautiful way to belong and live in the fullness of who we are made to be.[5]

The results of a 2022 HarperCollins study may not align with what you might have heard about deconstructors. The word we often hear is that people are abandoning the Christian faith and churches entirely, and that this is happening in droves. The churches are emptying out. They're collapsing, and it won't be long before everything falls apart. This study shows that 86 percent of book readers with profound shifts in how they view God and Christianity—those we might call deconstructors—have actually remained in the church.[6] It's not necessarily the *same* church, but nevertheless, *in* and not out. Nearly nine out of ten who underwent an intense renovation of their belief system remained engaged within the church at large. This contradicts the myth that those who are skeptical or filled with doubt—those flirting with deconstruction—are doing so out of a heart of rebellion or a desire to sin or justify sin in some way.

This myth is what social media at times calls "kayfabe," as in professional wrestling, where the wrestlers and audience enter into the performances as if they are reality. The idea of kayfabe suggests what the audience sees on the platform is staged, or at least the audience is going along with the show. For some in the audience, the performance is believable; for deconstructors, it's mockery.

Kayfabe won't work in religion. By the way, as Ryan Burge described in his book *20 Myths about Religion and Politics in America*, believable and attractive myths can circulate quickly.[7] Before long, many of these myths become established truths. What happens to deconstructors, we are suggesting, can be added to the myths.

Burge noted that the reasons for walking away have changed. Many of us know a friend who, because of entanglement in something the church generally considered sinful and worldly, ended up leaving the church (or getting pushed out) because of it. But today, people leave for very different reasons. Russell Moore explains it like this:

> When I first started in ministry, if someone came and said, "I'm losing my faith. I'm walking away from the church," the cause was almost always one of two things. Either the person started to find the supernatural incredible, or the person thought that the morality of the church was too strict in some way, usually having to do with sex. I almost never hear that anymore. . . . In many cases they're starting to question not whether the church is too strict but whether the church actually holds to a morality at all. What is alarming to me is that some of the people I find who are despairing are actually those who are the most committed to the teachings of Christianity.[8]

Stories like this one lead us to believe that the deconstruction crisis sweeping through the church is a prophetic movement of the Spirit born out of devotion to the way of Jesus—a Jesus many find invisible in churches.

Deconstruction is not easy. It is a painful and lonely path. But if you look closely, Jesus is still visible in the lives of those who experience its pain, confusion, loneliness, and fear. These are people who are *returning* to a version of the faith with renewed, if cautious, hope for God's people. They haven't abandoned the church; they love the church, even though they may not like their particular church or the one they grew up in.

A large percentage of those who have emerged on the other side of deconstruction have taken refuge in more liturgical forms of church, while others are branching out and tapping into denominations other than their own, something that may well have been discouraged in their upbringing. Others are finding their way to small churches, to house churches, or to alternative churches. For many, the hope they carry with them when they reenter the doors of the church gathering is not the hope of destruction, but the hope of resurrection. They hope the body of Christ will rise from the religious graveyard they are leaving behind.

Nine out of ten are still looking for a lot more Jesus. If they are leaving your denomination or church in droves, it might be time to consider why they don't see him there and why they have gone in search of this invisible Jesus elsewhere. Keep in mind that the deconstruction movement is not always an exodus from the faith. For many, deconstruction is not apostasy but a pilgrimage, not a departure from following Jesus but another step in the journey toward a Jesus-shaped way of life.

As we've talked with people, we've uncovered a few oddities. Here's one. We claim no numbers for this. No stats. It's just a hunch. But we think one of the reasons for the deconstruction some people are working through right now is Tom Wright. Yes, Tom Wright, known as N. T. Wright to some, the well-known New Testament scholar, Pauline theologian, and Anglican bishop. Why do we suggest this? Because Tom Wright was a leading proponent among a new generation of evangelicals of a *different* way of reading the Bible, along with a different framework for understanding Jesus and Paul, and a different set of ideas for thinking theologically. His books—especially the more popular ones like *Surprised by Hope*, *The Challenge of Jesus*, and *Simply Christian*—have stimulated a fresh appraisal of Jesus and a new spark of life for many. Many deconstructors we talked with have read him and tasted something new, and they don't want to go back to the fleshpots of evangelicalism.

Can we prove a connection? No, it's just a hunch. But there is something there, amiright? Here's another hunch—Dallas Willard. You, or someone you know, read one of his books on spiritual formation or listened to him at a conference. The response was to walk away and say, *There's something wrong in the church, and there's something more to the Christian life than what my church has to offer.* Or perhaps you were blown away by his *The Divine Conspiracy*, his powerful book about Jesus' vision for life as articulated in the Sermon on the Mount. Or perhaps it was Rachel Held Evans's *Faith Unraveled, A Year of Biblical Womanhood*, or *Inspired*. Other hunches need to include exposure to Brian McLaren's potent challenges to the church, like his *The Church on the Other Side* or *Generous Orthodoxy*. Far more often than not, Wright, Willard, Evans, and McLaren pointed their audiences toward a better faith, a more visible Jesus, and a church that did church as Jesus would have wanted.

This leads us to consider some of the repeated themes we pick up from those who are deconstructing. Here is an example from a woman named Lauren who provides some of her reasons for moving into deconstruction. Her reasons, please understand, are hardly unusual: · · · · · · · · · · ·

- Trying to convince my kids that are on the spectrum that certain nonsensical doctrines in fact "do" make sense and realizing that they would never buy it.
- Finding out the men at the top, with the most experience in Bible study were the most abusive.

- Being wounded and abandoned by church friends and held and healed by those "in the world."
- Reading church history books to discover heretic name calling over doctrinal differences and cognitive bias have been nonstop for centuries often ending in death.
- Listening to Bible scholars who didn't have an agenda and weren't groomed since childhood to believe one thing.

Lauren

Themes of Deconstruction

The themes we hear from those who are deconstructing their faith are not all that different from the questions and issues we wrestled with in our own deconstruction journeys. Yet while they may not be substantively different, they are *distinctive*. For each person working through deconstruction, there is a gravitas about what they undergo. We might call this the "deconstruction tunnel." And what drives them into the tunnel varies.

It might be the unmasking of immoral pastors and priests or the ridiculousness of making pseudoscientific claims about modern science, geology, and history on the basis of early chapters in Genesis, a book written thousands of years ago that has more in common with the "scientific" beliefs of ancient Babylon. Or they may have entered the tunnel because of what Christians have said about a God who seems to be sending the vast majority of human beings who have ever lived into eternal punishment in hell to experience fully conscious torment with no chance of turning back. Ever. They wonder, *How do I square that with a God of unconditional love?*

Others find the church unworthy of its claims because of what it has said about or how it has treated LGBTQ+ persons and those who support them, or how so many Christians have openly aligned their faith in Jesus with the Republican Party, either offering support for Donald J. Trump or failing to speak out against his outrageous statements. Or they have left because they know the January 6, 2021, riot on the US Capitol was inspired by many supposed Christians.

In short, they entered the dark tunnel of deconstruction because they refused to stand with others in the culture war of the last fifty years of evangelicalism. The symbols of this battle are well-known in the evangelical community: Bill Gothard, Quiverfull, Moral Majority, James Dobson, Douglas Wilson, homeschooling, purity rings, QAnon . . . and many more.[9]

They have left because evangelicalism has drawn its swords in the culture war, claiming to be on the defense and under attack by secularism, or claiming oppression and persecution over a legal matter, thereby creating an identity as the faithful remnant and the embattled minority. They have come to see the frightening truth that American evangelicalism needs an enemy in order to exist.[10] The routine "discovery" of a new enemy every few years serves the purposes of the culture war, keeping evangelicalism absorbed.

Yet the movement is perceived by many today as retrograde, and many would agree it has lost the war. Like those who believe the South will rise yet again, we still find those who wrongly think the culture war is still on. It's not. It's game, set, match. As evidence, consider this graph by Ryan Burge:

The most important (at least to evangelical culture warriors) sociomoral issues have all been lost: extramarital sex, abortion

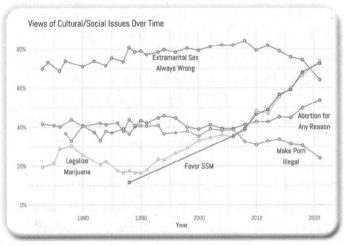

Views of Cultural/Social Issues Over Time

Ryan Burge (@ryanburge), Twitter, December 16, 2023, 10:40 a.m.

for any reason, making porn illegal, legalizing marijuana, and favoring same-sex marriage.

Yet the culture war is not the only reason people have left the church. We have heard stories of one woman after another who put the church in the rearview mirror because it has silenced the voices of women. "Why," they often ask, "should the work-place and public school be more committed to equality than the church?" The church claims it is at the leading edge of justice. Yet many women who know the viciousness of physical abuse hear at church a message of female submission to men. For these women, the church is not safe. Others leave, as Sara Billups has said, because "affiliating with Christianity in a progressive American city [Seattle] is not good for personal brand."[11] Why identify as a Christian when you have to spend your time constantly telling people, *But I'm not that kind of Christian*?

There is a way forward. It is not culture warring, but king-dom forming. The way of Jesus challenges his followers to form kingdom coalitions of persons who embody kingdom realities. Resistance to the way of the empire falls flat if it does not take shape in kingdom alternatives. Many deconstructors are forming some of the leading alternatives today.

One point of clarification is in order. We are not talking in this book about "fashionable deconstructors." Matt Chandler, a well-known American pastor, in a moment of pastoral insensitivity commented that "it's sexy to deconstruct." Yes, for some deconstructing is trendy. Even kayfabe. But that's not true for all. We would argue it's not true for many, as most are not engaging in this reexamination in order to hop on a trend. We care about those who look at the outside of a church and see glitz, who walk to the front of the auditorium, spot a platform, and then wander into the offices, open a door, and smell stink. We're talking about those who have walked the walk and talked the talk, and have gone inside the church doors far enough to know that Jesus is just not there anymore. They're the ones spotting the kayfabe. And it's because *they met Jesus, they know Jesus,* and *they want more Jesus.*

If it's sexy to deconstruct, as Chandler suggested, we'd say it's also sexy for some to criticize deconstructors. One Twitter (X) provocateur posted this tweet: • • • • • • • • • •

Ⓔ Eric — Aug 26

"Pastor, my theology has changed since going to college. I can't trust the Bible anymore."

"Really? How long have you been having sex with your girlfriend?"

Deconstruction and doubt are often thinly veiled fig leaves attempting to cover lives of sexual immorality.

Sexy indeed.

To his credit, Chandler came back to explain what he didn't mean and what he did mean, and we quote from his more pastorally sensitive approach:

> Deconstruction doesn't mean doubt or theological wrestle or struggling through church hurt. . . . I have the deepest empathy and compassion for those who find themselves wading in those waters. I certainly don't want to make things harder for anyone in those seasons and struggles. I've journeyed through all three of those spaces in my 30 years of following after Jesus. If that's where you are I think you're going to get to the other side and see Jesus as more beautiful than you previously imagined. . . . That's the way I'm praying.[12]

We are too. We care about those who are in these deep waters. We do not think it wise to sneer, as many do today, at the Nones, Dones, Nonverts, or Deconstructors. Rather, we are called to listen, and to listen well enough to learn, because they have much to teach us. As a pastor and professor who has specialized in doubt and deconstruction said after a young man burst into tears in his office after pouring out his heart's discontent, "All I could give him was my full, undivided attention. Welcome to the age of deconstruction."[13]

There is a prophetic voice here that has been silenced by many church leaders. Instead of conducting painful exit interviews with the throngs of people leaving churches today, these church leaders have never heard why they are leaving or sought to understand what makes deconstructors tick. Or perhaps they don't want to hear because making an adjustment would require a revolution of the soul.

My (Scot's) own reasons for deconstructing the faith I was nurtured into were different from current deconstructors, but not significantly different. My deconstruction journey was provoked by my firsthand experience with American fundamentalism (before many moved away from that term and began calling it "evangelicalism," which was then labeled in a degrading manner as "neo-evangelicalism" by some fundamentalists) by reading the likes of Francis Schaeffer, who tossed fire on the dry timbers of the American church; Ray Stedman, who convinced me church should be a body life of spiritual gifts; and Dietrich Bonhoeffer, who convinced me that much of what I had learned looked more like cheap than costly grace. Encounters with these heady ideas led me into a process of deconstructing until all I knew at that period of my life was *what I did not believe*. If I were to continue with Jesus, I had to *re*construct my faith.

There are, of course, many dangers associated with deconstruction. If you're drawn to its vibe, it opens you to a load of criticism and, at times, can lead to cynicism. True enough. It's easier to find problems than to create solutions, and to propose solutions than to implement them into flourishing transformations. One criticism of the church can lead you to others, and before long, you're armed with a heavy briefcase full of problems aimed at the church. But finding a solution is still important. You might not have any for months or even years. But we encourage you to carry on in the hope of a better faith.

The Only "Solution" Worth Exploring

The first class I (Scot) took in seminary, which met at 7:45 a.m. in a dingy, big classroom with a smelly carpet, was called "The

Synoptic Gospels." The professor was a good man named Walter Liefeld. In that class, I experienced the beginning of my awakening, and while it took about a decade for that awakening to fill me with light, it began there. I walked away from that class a changed person attached to three simple convictions:

1. I had grown up in a kind of Christian faith where Jesus was not a person.
2. I encountered Jesus in that class.
3. I wanted a faith centered on Jesus.

In my past, Jesus was a cross, an agent, a Savior, a resurrection, and eternal life. He got me from "point sin" to "point salvation." But he was just an idea, invisible and esoteric—not a living, breathing, teaching, compassionate, loving Galilean Jew who performed astounding miracles and made shocking statements about the leaders and profoundly egocentric statements about himself. He functioned more like a mascot, something to be a fan of, not a person to embody. Later in life, I read these lines, and they jumped off the page. These lines so perfectly describe the one true witness who changed my life in seminary:

> The most vital thing is to meet this person, listen to this person, get to know this person, trust this person, follow this person, converse with this person, relate continually to this person, be loved and love this person. All else flows from this. And the most fundamental thing to know is that Jesus is as God is.[14]

I wanted to get to know this Jesus, so I concentrated on Jesus in my studies, my academic degrees, and what eventually became my career as a professor and writer. Jesus' Sermon on the Mount became the text that fundamentally reshaped my faith, and I studied it daily all summer long during seminary. I pondered deeply what Jesus said about discipleship and put together so many notes they became the basis for lectures I gave as a young professor. I became fascinated with how the Gospel of Matthew presents Jesus, especially from the end of chapter 4 through chapter 10. Those chapters define who Jesus is for me.

Almost no one enters the tunnel of deconstructing their Christian faith because of Jesus. They enter into the darkness of that tunnel because of an experience with the church, because of something the church teaches, or because of an experience with individual Christians. Many in the tunnel of deconstruction, and even those beyond the tunnel, consider themselves passionate followers of Jesus, even more committed than before. But they may no longer be members of a church.

To put it bluntly, many are in the tunnels of deconstruction because they have read Jesus and they want *more* Jesus. They're with Jesus in the tunnel of deconstruction. A. J. Swoboda, who has written and spoken of his own decade-long deconstruction, put it this way: deconstructors "have tasted Jesus, and rigid religion has proven to be a poor substitute." Swoboda urges his readers to "read Jesus and tell me he isn't worth following."[15] He's right. Emma, a deconstructor, wrote, after a serious period of deconstruction, "I feel like I couldn't get rid of Christianity altogether. . . . I do want to rediscover my faith and I do want to continue to walk with Jesus in some way."[16]

Deconstructors today have more to disagree with than I did when I was in that place. Yet the process is much the same. It involves leaving one's faith community, one in which many of us were nurtured and in which we have many close friends, an experience that undercuts the social and relational pillars of life. It takes courage to do this, and that courage pushes me to admiration at times.

Yet what I admire even more is the courage to reconstruct one's faith on the basis of Jesus alone.

3 Interlude: Three Phases of Deconstruction

(Leading to a Centered-Set Jesus Faith)

> **Ⓚ Kurtis — Jul 22**
>
> Mine [my deconstruction] started when I was young.
> The words weren't matching the actions of the leaders.
> The God that humbled and serves was being used to
> extort and control others. It got worse as I got deeper
> into ministry and leadership. I challenged with love, I got
> exiled and slandered.

D-words matter—words like *deconstruction, disengagement, differentiation, disentanglement, doubt, despair, dejection, disillusionment, dissatisfaction, discontentment, disgruntlement,* and *disenchantment.* These words matter because they describe the genuine experiences of many Christians today. Our goal is not just to understand their words, but to understand them as people. What happened? Why? When? And where are they headed now? We make no claim to represent them all. Nor do we know all of their concerns. Deconstructors cannot be simply profiled. We hope to represent some of them and some of their biggest concerns in this book. But we are not sociologists with demographics and statistics mapped on spreadsheets in our book bags.

Maybe you've landed among the D-words. We hear you, and more often than not, we think you've illuminated problems within the church with your questions. Some of you are prophets about the profits and the partisanship of the church. We have watched and have sought to understand. And based on what we've heard from you (and seen for ourselves), we would describe three phases in the deconstruction process.

Some people enter into phase one or even phase two, but then end up back where they were before. Some enter into phase one and two, and days later, they have left the faith altogether. Most people we've known enter deconstruction's phases gently and gradually. It's like watching the evening shade move across the front lawn. Some arrive at the other end—if they ever arrive—changed, transformed, and no longer willing to go back. Some go through periods of anger and bitter resentment. Others chill their way through it all. Most experience a mix. The tunnel of deconstruction can last weeks, months, or even years. Some are always deconstructing and reconstructing. Some are not even aware they have been in the tunnel for a long time.

Deconstruction is costly—costing a person's status, respect in a group, community, friends, family, and perhaps even a job and income. It can affect their past, present, and future. And most people we've talked with don't consciously choose to deconstruct. Instead, they find themselves in the deconstruction tunnel because they discover (and not always immediately, at the conscious level) their deep, unanswered questions. They are deeper than just annoying; they are gnawing, soul-quivering questions. In the tunnel, they realize that their own spiritual and intellectual integrity rises up and must be consciously acknowledged and respected. They find they cannot *not* have these questions. They know they must face them—and then figure out where to go next.

Phases of Deconstruction

Deconstruction is, at the most basic level, a rethinking of one's faith. Some people are convinced the acts of rethinking what they believe and questioning those beliefs are sinful. Some teach that the heart is desperately wicked and deceitful, always desiring the wrong thing (except what some authority decides you should want). You may have learned from church authorities that you can't trust yourself or your questions, therefore trusting your own gut and asking questions must be deconstructing.

When you are taught that the heart and mind are too corrupt for you to trust, it makes you think deconstruction is inherently dangerous. But here is our first pushback; it's not. In fact, it's normal. And it's even more normal for those with an inclination toward the theoretical, philosophical, historical, or psychological. The entire Protestant tradition is based on two major reconstructors—Martin Luther and John Calvin. (We could add lesser-known names from among the Anabaptists, like Menno Simons.) The Protestant tradition teaches *semper reformanda*—which means "always reforming"—and all "reforming" begins with some deconstructing.

And notice that those who say you can't trust yourself sure seem to think you can trust *them*. That's because they think they can trust themselves. We believe that by pushing back against those who advocate for this kind of blind trust in authority is doing the proper and good work of deconstruction.

Reasons for Leaving the Church

We are willing to hang our hats on the hook that those who leave the church but remain committed do so because Jesus has become too invisible in churches. They leave because the salvation and healing they need and the love that cultivates true flourishing are neither seen nor felt in the body of Christ. We see this as the crux of the issue. We want to be clear that our focus in this book is on the pastoral need to hear the prophetic voice of deconstructors. We're also aware that there are many other reasons (both prophetic and not) for people leaving the church.

In their book *The Great Dechurching*, Jim Davis and Michael Graham, with help from Ryan Burge, unpack their research on why people leave the church. In their study, they carve up the dechurched into (1) cultural Christians, (2) mainstream evangelicals, (3) exvangelicals, (4) BIPOC (black, indigenous, and persons of color), and (5) mainline Protestants and Roman Catholics.

Here are a few reasons each group leaves the church:[1]

Cultural Christians. Friends don't attend; regular involvement is inconvenient; suffering changed my view of God; I'm sensitive to gender identity criticisms; I moved to a new community; church is too restrictive of sexual freedom; I'm turned off by scandals involving clergy; I worship online; the sermons aren't relevant; I see racism there; I have other priorities; I doubt God's goodness; I doubt God's existence.

Mainstream evangelicals. I moved to a new community; regular involvement is inconvenient; I've experienced divorce, remarriage, or family change; COVID-19 got me out of the habit; I didn't fit in with the congregation; I didn't experience love in the congregation.

Exvangelicals. I didn't fit in with the congregation; I moved to a new community; I didn't experience love from the congregation; regular involvement is inconvenient; I had negative experiences in an evangelical church; I'm turned off by the politics of the congregation; I no longer believed what the congregation believed; I disagreed with the politics of the clergy.

BIPOC. Here, the research was broken down into those eighteen to twenty-five years old and those twenty-six to thirty-nine years old.

Eighteen to twenty-five. I didn't fit in with the congregation; I had other priorities; I've had bad experiences in the church; my college education caused me to question my faith; there was a lack of people my age; I've had bad experiences with evangelicals; I wanted to explore my sexuality.

Twenty-six to thirty-nine. I didn't fit in with the congregation; I found community online or at work; I wanted to enjoy the benefits of surplus finances; there was a lack of people my age; my faith was not my own but borrowed from my family; I've had bad experiences with evangelicals; I've had bad experiences in my church; I had other priorities.

Mainline Protestants and Roman Catholics.

Mainline. I moved to a new community; I had other priorities for my time and money; I didn't fit in with the congregation; the politics of the congregation; I doubt God's existence; regular involvement is inconvenient; I've experienced divorce, remarriage, or a family change; I didn't experience love in the congregation.

Roman Catholic. I had other priorities for my time and money; the politics of the congregation; I'm turned off by the politics of the clergy; I didn't fit in with the congregation; I moved to a new community; faith just wasn't working for me; I'm turned off by scandals involving clergy; I've experienced divorce, remarriage, or a family change.

Liminality

For some, deconstruction is a halfway house for confining church experiences and doctrines—a time of release, preparation, and eventually resocialization. Those in this first stage may say they have had negative church experiences, but they are still convinced the church ought to be something different and better.

Perhaps you can relate. You may feel you can no longer be genuinely and authentically present in a church. You can't participate in the systemic direction of a church. Its precious doctrines now annoy you. *Who cares about the rapture when the existential, deeply personal reality of a living faith is what got raptured?* You see participation of any sort as a form of hypocrisy and complicity. You may now think of Sunday-go-to-meeting church behavior as something in your rearview mirror. For you, there is no more pretending. You have become a dissident of the system.

At this point, you know what you *don't* believe more than what you *do* believe. With respect to the church, we would describe this as being in a liminal space, a space between faith and no faith. Many who are in this phase are ambiguous and anxious, wounded and wondering. You may have family and friends who are worried about you, but you may feel a callous disregard for their worries because you are worried about them. It can also be a confusing time, since you don't always know where to locate yourself.[2]

The sense many people have at this stage is like playing Jenga. You have gone around a circle of players three times and lots of blocks have been removed. The tower is a bit wobbly. You sense that if you pull out this block or that block, the whole thing might suddenly come tumbling down. But you aren't sure.

This sense of the unknown keeps you in that liminal space. You may still stand among the familiar, surrounded by people you have a history with (some good, some bad), but it is a history you *know* and can navigate. Beyond the familiar, however, the liminal space of the unknown stands empty and vast. You have heard others discrediting those who live there, beyond the borders of your familiar world.

Some people may remain in liminality for years, others for most of their lives, never fully vocalizing the dissonance they see for fear of making ripples that might turn into waves and drown them. They know they risk being cast from fellowship and tarnishing their reputation with gossip and accusations. And so they stay. They stand on the edge of faith, looking out into the distance for something or someone they can cling to. At times it feels like they are clinging to a buoy in a terrifying ocean storm. Some, to be sure, are cock-a-hoop about leaving the faith and the church—excited to party and celebrate their newfound freedoms from religious obligations. But most don't. Most ponder. And wonder.

In this phase of liminality, all it takes is one person to set them free. Most persons in liminality aren't driven to the edge of faith merely by something they've read. Information doesn't change humans; incarnation does. Instead, you meet someone who, by divine chance, shares your questions, and you observe that they hold different doctrines without anxiety and without a collapse of their faith. Or you meet someone who is Christlike, who may also embrace people your church has rejected. They aren't strapped down by a limited, fundamentalist reading of the Bible or by a worldview that rejects established science. Or the someone you encounter may subscribe to a different political ideology and they don't hate God, as you were assured they would. Regardless, when the embodied representative of your (former) Other steps forth and earns your respect, you inevitably gain strength in your own *liminality* to courageously continue your journey out of tradition toward Jesus.

An important takeaway for the church as we listen and learn from those in this first stage of deconstruction is that *incarnation matters*. Jesus must be made visible. Those who earn the respect of the people asking questions, facing doubts, and entering the tunnel of deconstruction will end up illuminating their path forward.

My (Tommy) first step out of the place of liminality happened the day I found out that one of the elders in my church, a generous and Christlike man who made Jesus visible for me, believed in evolution (scandalous!). He dropped a comment about it one day in casual conversation, as if it wasn't a controversial subject in our conservative church. I was astounded. "You believe in evolution?" I asked, to which he simply said, "Of course! You want a drink from the fridge?"—as though he hadn't said anything unusual at all.

I had grown up in the CCM (Contemporary Christian Music) scene, listening to songs about the evils of evolution. There was a Stephen Curtis Chapman song from the early 1990s about two children standing up against a deceived teacher who was teaching them evolution.[3] Another song by Geoff Moore & The Distance making a mockery of evolution and the teachers who taught it.[4] Christian media had successfully indoctrinated me to see anyone who believed evolution as openly rebellious or, at the very least, immoral.

But this man was neither of those things. He was Christlike, and his embodiment of the Christian faith had a powerful effect on me. Incarnation is effective. That's why God chose to employ it in the person of Christ Jesus. Jesus—what he said, what he did, and, even more, who he was and is today—compels those in a place of liminality to continue seeking.

Elimination

As a deconstructor, you may have discarded or are still discarding elements of the doctrines and teachings of your church or certain beliefs your parents and other trusted teachers taught you. These may include doctrines such as creationism, dispensationalism, Christian nationalism, inerrancy, original sin, evangelism (as it is commonly practiced), or any number of doctrinal beliefs. It could also include nondoctrinal matters—goofy things like not reading Harry Potter, wearing a purity ring, not listening to heavy rock, not getting tattoos, or even not going to jujitsu lessons. Or it could be something you were taught about the evils of voting Democrat, the un-American-ness of being a pacifist, or the idealism of rejecting the death penalty. Maybe you saw the label of "feminist" applied to people who were totally rejected.

Sometimes you will decide to jettison particular Christian and sub-Christian doctrines or practices because they are additions to the faith—cultural baggage, something held only because your tribe affirms them and not because they are inherent to following Jesus. That's normal. If that's where you or someone you know is at, you or they are entering a new phase. Now you not only know what you *don't* believe; you have decisively set some doctrines aside. You may decide to tell your friends and family, "I'm no longer an evangelical," "I don't affirm the institutional church," or "Church leadership is nothing but a power game." You are rejecting some of what you once believed and gaining footholds for a more bracing belief. You don't know if your faith will survive this period of elimination or if you will remain a Christian, at least in the way your tradition defines it. This may concern you more than you care to admit, but going back is not an option.

In this phase, a deconstructor has not left the faith, nor have they given up on church. Yet they are so "de-constructive" in their interactions with the church and other Christians that they have a hard time participating in any positive way in the life of a church.

This phase of deconstruction is known for its intensive searching. Searchers have questions—often more questions than they have answers. And some of those questions are more than questions. They are answer-questions, like, *Have you noticed how little our church cares about the poor? Or war? Or race? Or greed?* Perhaps you are reading a book or conversing with others who are also asking questions as you look for a new vision. You may find a freshness in someone like Tom Wright, resonate with Anthea Butler's scathing commentary on society, or discover something satisfying, even mystical, in Richard Rohr. You are searching for the gold of Jesus and an authentic Christian expression, but you don't know exactly where it will be found. You can be easily irritated, even angry, and not a little bit cynical. Most of the people we encounter today who say they are in a deconstruction phase in their faith are in the "delete this, delete that" mode.

Those who have not struggled at a deep level with their faith identity are likely to accuse those working through this process of doctrinal elimination of "throwing out their faith." But this is not entirely accurate. Those in this phase are not throwing out their faith or on some invisible slippery slope. They may not even be walking away from the church, Christianity, or their faith. Instead, they are jettisoning the stumbling blocks that are keeping them from truly believing in Jesus. If this is where you're at, you may feel like you are clearing away the rubble. Wiping off generations of dust. Scraping the scum off the pond.

Liberation

Many deconstructors eventually find a new way forward. When you break into this third phase, you feel free. You still think about your old church, but that time is clearly in your past. At times you miss elements of that church, but you are on a new path, finding freedom to think what you think, do what you do, and feel what you feel. Best of all, you are doing it without those familiar stumbling blocks on your path. These new ways of liberation differ as much as the diversity we find in our world. As one of the "liberated," you have no desire to go back to the cages, to the chains, or to the walls that formerly confined you in your faith.

We offer these descriptions to help unpack some of the nuances among those who are leaving religion behind but still seeking Jesus. They are looking for the Jesus who is missing from their church—the invisible Jesus. But we also offer a word of caution because no stereotyping of deconstructors fully fits. So forget about finding one that will cover every person and every scenario.

Some of those who fret about deconstruction in our churches want a simplistic theory that explains it all, but there is none. Underneath it all, the best we can say is that *deconstructors find the complexities of the Christian faith as they have experienced it in a family, a church community, or a circle of trusted voices to be inadequate.* For them, the complexities have been oversimplified, and the answers to their questions are inadequate. They are tired of simplicities; they are done with them. Whether it is an intellectual problem (e.g., the apostle Paul seeming to silence women, gruesome theories about hell), the problem of hypocrisy (e.g., well-known pastors who are morally compromised on the basis of their own teachings), or a social problem (e.g., Why can't the church get on board with universal healthcare?), they know the church falls short. The confident credibility of the church's claims withers their faith. As one parent shared with me the other day, "My son is *so over* the whole church thing." This parent is a Christian leader, but she thinks her son is onto something vital.

We do too.

Your past is inadequate. The days of accepting the answers you were given are behind you. You are searching for the meaning of life. And you are not afraid of Jesus. No, you aren't disappointed with or disengaged from Jesus. Jesus remains your heart and soul, but you think he has been lost in the morass of institutions, theories, requirements, competitions, and Christian celebrities. To borrow from the title of Dan Kimball's book, you "like Jesus but not the church."[5]

Please know that if the description we've been unpacking fits you, we are not trying to persuade you to abandon your journey. Instead, in the pages that follow, we want to sketch a view of Jesus, a *re*construction that avoids the trappings of institutions and has the potential to start you on a new path on your journey further into the kingdom of God.

In this book we're exploring most of the eight rediscoveries discussed by Meghan Good:

1. Jesus is the authoritative lens through which God is seen and the Bible is interpreted.
2. Salvation encompasses the setting right of all things, on earth as it is in heaven.

3. A Christian is one who acknowledges Jesus as Lord and follows him in life and death.
4. A new community is both the means and goal of God's transformational activity.
5. Jesus' people are sent as ambassadors for God's reconciling work.
6. The Spirit guides and resources God's mission.
7. Evil is overcome by the power of sacrificial love.
8. The unity of the church is secured by the center it orbits.[6]

Jesus Is the Center

Some have described what's happening in deconstruction as a kind of "centered-set" thinking.[7] Time and time again, we've found that deconstructors want to get back to Jesus and want to base everything they believe on Jesus. They often describe a sensation of discovering the Bible all over again when they begin to read the Gospels once again. They describe a shift to thinking more like Jesus, acting more like Jesus, and letting Jesus' vision for the kingdom reshape their life. He becomes the center of their life.

Centered-set thinking contrasts more directly with *bounded-set* thinking. A bounded set emphasizes boundaries. It defines who is "in" and who is "out." It spells out in detail what an acceptable person must believe and how such persons should behave. Only those who are inside the boundaries can belong to the group. Uniformity characterizes the group, and the uniformity is conservative in the sense that it is neither flexible nor open to change. Either you're in or you're out, and if you're in, you're all in.

The common problem with bounded sets is determining how to define the boundaries. A bounded-set person could risk losing Jesus in their efforts to build walls at the borders of their faith. Deconstructors would say those who think this way have lost Jesus because they focus excessively on who is in and who is out, and especially on keeping the wrong people out.

Centered-set thinking defines a person not by a set of boundaries but by their relationship or proximity to the center of the faith (which is Jesus). A centered-set person tends to focus their attention on the magnificence at the core of their faith. The centered-set person perceives people, behaviors, and ideas not by a set of fences but by their proximity or likeness to Jesus. Are they moving toward Jesus, toward the center? Instead of uniformity and inflexibility, the centered set tends to have diversity, room for adjustments, and a toleration of differences as people approach Jesus in different ways from different directions. Generally speaking, centered sets are dynamic, while bounded sets are more static.

A centered-set approach to faith does not mean the only article of faith is Jesus, and Jesus alone. Beliefs about God, the Spirit, redemption, the cross, resurrection, justification by faith, and other beliefs are all still important in a centered-set approach. But rather than defining the faith with clear boundary markers, we have something more akin to what C. S. Lewis called *mere Christianity*.[8]

There is a defined center, but it is Jesus, the person, the one who lived and taught and did astounding things, who died and was raised and ascended and who is returning. The stories in the Gospels and our theological affirmations derive from who Jesus is and what Jesus did, and they are the ones that matter. The less connected these are to Jesus, the less centered they are. And we don't get to decide for ourselves which items to pick and choose. This is not the "You choose atonement, but I don't like atonement" approach. A centered set may be less clearly defined, but it is *not* a "you do you and I do me" form of the faith.

I (Tommy) recently met with a woman who left her church a week before our conversation. Recounting her faith journey, she shared, "By the time I was nineteen or so, I realized there was no place for me in this particular tradition, although I was still very much into Jesus and I loved reading theology."

Let's pause for a second and first notice that the modern American church, with all its cultural accommodations, has become the kind of place where young women who love Jesus and theology no longer feel welcome. That's a tragedy, no matter how we dress it up.

This woman went on to tell me she has been "overwhelmed by the amount of people my age who have also deconstructed and ultimately lost their faith." While listening to her, my first thought was that those who left could have come together as a fresh expression of church; instead, they are wandering through a spiritual wilderness, looking for signs of God on the horizon. Many of them carry the label of *agnostic*, not because they think God doesn't exist, but because it is how they were raised to describe their current condition of "not knowing."

Those who were raised in theological structures that emphasized certainty know what this feels like. There is no room to question, no place for the one who might admit, "I don't know." Again, we find that many today know far more about what they *no longer* believe than what they *do* believe, but they are still on a journey. They're thinking and talking, and if we are wise, we will be listening.

On the other side of this struggle with *a-gnosticism* (not knowing), many have rediscovered the communion of the saints. We might call this the co-journey of pilgrims toward Jesus Christ. And when you find this communion, the *a* in agnosticism begins to fall away and you finally begin to *know* Jesus instead of simply practicing a religion. Those in this place are often surprised to rediscover the *Spirit* of God.

I (Tommy) met a man one Sunday who was on his journey back from deconstruction to reconstruction. He came up to me after the sermon and said, "It was surprising to hear you speak of the Holy Spirit. I grew up in a conservative tradition and then deconstructed and have been gathering with a local community that doesn't believe that stuff anymore—the divinity, the spiritual realm, all that." Then he admitted, "But I've been deconstructing *that* as well, and it's been so long since I've pondered the Spirit. It's nice to hear you talk about it again."

We have found that the Spirit is present and active around the table with followers of Jesus who seek Christlikeness together and lay down roots in fresh ways as new expressions of Christ's body in the world. This is the *liberation* we speak of in this book—freedom to lay down culturally burdened forms of Christianity for a more Jesus-formed, Spirit-shaped faith.

Losing Jesus in Our Politics

No two stories of deconstruction are identical. Lots of deconstructors never even use or embrace the term deconstruction. And not all deconstructors become reconstructors. The majority do, however. One of those who, so far as I have read, does not use the term "deconstruction" is Jon Ward, the *Yahoo! News* chief national correspondent for politics. Ward came to faith and was nurtured under the teaching of C. J. Mahaney, pastor of Covenant Life Church (and now known as Sovereign Grace Churches). The path before him was clearly designed—his politics were set to be right wing; his theology would be the new Calvinism of John Piper and Wayne Grudem; and his spirituality would be an intense form of religious experience. Until they weren't.

Ward slowly but surely drifted away from this world. He learned the subtle art of critical thinking and the disinterested interrogation that is characteristic of journalists. He was married and had children, yet all the while he was deconstructing and wondering what was on the other side of faith. At one point in his journey, Ward expressed a longing for clarity that so many of us are familiar with. Ward came to terms with the wounds he received in his church tradition, but also wrestled with one of the central questions in the journey of deconstruction: *What do I now believe?*

> In the summer of 2019, I took my daughter out for breakfast on her birthday. Then we walked along the beach, exploring the coastline, picking up rocks, and taking photos. It was a beautiful day. At one point, I looked out at the ocean, wondering what I still believed in. The previous few years had called so much into question. So many people I'd trusted and looked up to had fallen short. So many assumptions I'd held had been shown to be faulty. Everything was up for reexamination. I did not want to mislead my children. What could I tell them that I knew was true, and what could I tell them that I hoped was true? Where did knowledge end and where did faith begin?[1]

Did you catch that? *Everything was up for reexamination.* Not one item, not two items of faith. *Everything.* That line hits like a trumpet blast for us. Many can relate to that *everything. Everything*, however, can be unnerving.

Ward probes for solid ground in the midst of his bewilderment over the inconsistency of Jesus' kingdom vision and what he had observed about the Christians around him:

> I looked at the sky, the water, the trees. I believed that a Creator was behind all of this. That was something. Beyond that, however, I wasn't in much of a mood to make many declarative

statements. There was so much to wonder about after the past few years, so much unsettled and so much exposed. We had friends who thought my wife and I were questioning parts of our faith because of things that had happened in our churches growing up. They seemed to have no clue that it was their triumphalist use of faith mixed with materialism and support for politicians who demonized poor and minority people that was part of the reason that the Christian faith had become questionable to us. Increasingly, we saw that they and so many other American Christians who talked and sang loudly about their love for Jesus seemed to be living lives that did not share Jesus' concerns.

Ward taps into something that many deconstructors also experience. He challenges the certainty many Christians have that they are on the straight and narrow:

To struggle toward truth, to refuse easy answers, and to remain in a place where uncertainty and complexity present ongoing challenges—that seems closer to what Jesus would want.

He then probes deeper into what he now believes:

My family and my work give me purpose and meaning. My friends ground me. When it comes to faith, some days I feel purpose. Other days I feel lost, or unsure. But I'm not in a hurry to figure it out. That point, it seems, is to be honest in the pursuit and true to the most basic teachings of the faith: to love God, to love those around you, and to lift up the downtrodden. . . .

My faith has been sparked by seeing that the real Jesus beckons me to follow him into a life of vulnerability that threatens the false gods of comfort and ease. Like many others, I'm trying to figure out how to walk that path. It's daunting and scary, and most days I feel like I'm not doing a very good job. But it does at least have the ring of truth.

Few of those going through a reexamination process can write like Jon Ward, who at times has the syntax and structure of Earnest Hemingway. But he deftly puts into words the experience of so many deconstructors. Like so many others, Ward is looking for Jesus.

At the beginning of chapter 3, we mentioned a number of D-words that matter because they define the experiences of many Christians—words like *deconstruction, disengagement, differentiation, disentanglement, doubt, despair, dejection, disillusionment, dissatisfaction, discontentment, disgruntlement,* and *disenchantment.* One or more of those words may be your word for the year. "Religion," Bob Smietana wrote, "is only as good as the people who practice it."[2] When a religion and its doctrines lead people to the D-words, it's a sign the professionals, pastors, professors, and people who practice that religion are not practicing it well enough.

Looking for a Place Where Jesus Is the Great I Am

We've been listening to deconstructors for more than a decade, and one consistent message we have heard is just how important Jesus is to them. Many will flat out say Jesus is their Lord, even if they think it's cringey to parrot what institutional Christians say. I (Scot) taught college students for seventeen years, and many were among the finest Christians I have ever met. Some of them confessed they no longer went to church, but they were always quick to add, "Not because I'm not a Christian. Not because I don't follow Jesus." In fact, more than one person said, "*Because* I follow Jesus, I don't go to church."

What we learned from them in their deconstruction and reconstruction phases of faith was that they believed their church attendance kept them from following Jesus. So what did they do instead? They served the homeless. They spoke out against injustice. They prayed and read the Prophets and the Gospels. They met with a few other followers of Jesus. They did these things *because* they followed Jesus. The churches they knew were filled with church attenders and admirers of Jesus, but not real Jesus followers. And whether they were right or wrong, they thought they could discern the difference. They told me they wanted a Jesus-first religion, not a church-first religion. So they chose to follow Jesus and left the church.

A Jesus-first way of life was all the first followers of Jesus knew. They knew no other way. The Gospel of John informed its readers that Jesus performed an astounding miracle by turning "five small barley loaves and two small fish" into food for five thousand men.[3] Since the women and children were not counted, we can assume that some ten to fifteen thousand people were there. If you think there is some serious exaggeration at work in this account, you would not be alone. What is not an exaggeration is the reality that Jesus is someone who does *astounding things*.

And the incidents that came next were no less astounding. In the middle of that event, Jesus made a claim far greater than any claim spoken by any person. Ever. Then, after feeding all those people, after collecting the leftovers that were more than the original loaves and fishes, and after pushing his disciples out onto the Sea of Galilee to get away from it all—after all this, a storm broke out, and the disciples were scared witless and rowed like madmen to outrun the storm.

Four miles out from shore, Jesus showed up. Barefoot surfing without a board or a sail. They saw him, and they were scared. And then Jesus spoke to them. Many translations render his words as, "It is I," but the Common English Bible gets it exactly right: "I Am."[4]

Do you know what "I Am" evoked in Jesus' world? The divine name—I AM WHO I AM—found in the book of Exodus.[5] When Moses wanted to know God's name so he could go back and tell all the Israelites about a crazy plan to liberate them from Egypt, he asked God, "Who do I tell them sent me?" And God replied, "I Am Who I Am. So say to the Israelites, 'I Am has sent me to you.'"

But don't just take our word for it. One of the world's great scholars, Richard Bauckham, also thinks there is more going on here than we typically see. These I Am statements cannot have the ordinary meaning (it's me), but instead they point to divine identity, which evokes God's "claim to unique and exclusive divinity." Or, Jesus is "unambiguously identifying himself with the one and only God."[6]

Here's a quick summary of what we think is happening: God told Moses that God was the I Am. Israel's prophets spoke of God as the I Am.[7] And then, unlike Moses or the prophet Isaiah, Jesus looked at that name, thought about that name, thought about himself, and then flat out appropriated the I Am language *for himself*. Often. That's a big leap. Everything about the Christian faith depends on Jesus being the I Am. What it means is this:

Jesus reveals God.

Jesus is God.

The God of Christians looks like, or ought to look like, Jesus.

When Jesus goes invisible, God does too.

This is where many start. Knowing Jesus is God forms the foundation for their deconstruction. Why? Because deconstructors are not playing games. They are pleading with the church to remember who their God really is. To remember that God is Jesus and Jesus is God.

We are asking you if you believe that a Galilean man, Jesus of Nazareth, could think of himself this way and then tell others. We are asking you if you know a place where this kind of Jesus is present. Is this the Jesus people will meet each time your church, small group, or church board gathers together? It's not primarily about what you experienced as a church or learned in your church. I Am says Jesus ought to be front, middle, center, left, right, bottom, and top of everything the church says and does. All day long. Every week.

If Jesus has made such a claim, why have churches and institutions moved so far away from Jesus that he is all but invisible in their midst? In many churches today, one barely hears about Jesus or observes people centering their lives on him. How can we end up so deep in our religion that we lose Jesus? The religion *of* Jesus is first and foremost a religion *about* Jesus.

And this is why we need to listen to deconstructors. If Jesus is to be the center of our churches, and people are leaving because it's not a reality, then maybe they're saying something we need to hear. Can we really blame them for wanting a place where Jesus can be found?

"Where Have All the Guides Gone?"

It's fairly common for someone entering their mid-thirties to mid-forties to look around for a person who has walked life's journey before them, weathered the storms, and navigated the struggles, and come out intact, faithful, and maintaining joy and love for God and others.

Before the great unveiling (the apocalypse) of the last decade, such older persons weren't hard to find. There were many wonderful older and wiser people—professors, parents, pastors, religious leaders, authors, speakers, even politicians—to whom younger Christians looked for inspiration. Those younger Christians could imagine a future where they would provide wisdom for those who walked in their footprints after them.

But since 2015, many of those wonderful older and wiser people we looked to for wisdom have eroded their witness through promotion of political extremism, conspiracy theories, and election lies. They have stirred up fear of gay and transgender people. Those willing to listen have heard young people share how much their parents have changed in recent years. "It's like COVID-19 and lockdowns scrambled their brains. We don't even recognize them anymore!" one said to me (Tommy). Several people in my church have watched their parents turn against the gracious, loving Christlike ways of their old life and go all in on Trumpism. They've changed, enticed by the allure of power and control, always angling for an argument, and often spewing propaganda and spreading lies about their political enemies.

It seems evangelicalism has aligned itself—married itself, if you will—to the Republican Party. Four out of five evangelicals vote Republican, and partisan politics is closely correlated to the growth of the Nones and the Dones. Many deconstructors have left the evangelical house in recent years because they have learned that Democrats are no longer welcome. Sociologists are discovering, somewhat surprisingly, that American evangelicals do not choose their political party on the basis of their religion; they choose their church or their faith expression on the basis of their politics. Ryan Burge noted:

> Recent scholarship seems to be pointing more and more to an understanding of politics as the first cause and religious affiliation lying downstream from that. Instead of deciding who they will cast a ballot for based on their religious tradition, most Americans pick a church that lines up with their view of the political world. . . .
>
> As evangelicals have become more linked to one political party, that has naturally led to the alienation of a lot of people who think differently about politics.[8]

If we fail to see a problem here, we are likely part of the problem. The co-opting of evangelicals by partisan politics was always a Faustian bargain, just another form of idolatry. And some readers would likely say it goes both ways. Yes, it surely does. But the mainline Protestants who align with Democrats are not the ones claiming to be Bible-based Christians. Our concern is that Bible-based Christians have surrendered their hearts to dance with those in political power.

No one has described (mocked?) this alignment of evangelicals with the GOP more cleverly than Tony Keddie:

Republican Jesus is a Christian, white, working-class carpenter who was born in Israel a long, long time ago. His mom wasn't ready to have a baby, but she was prolife and had a good, hard-working man by her side, so it turned out just fine. After legally immigrating to Egypt for a short time, Republican Jesus and his parents pulled themselves up by their sandal-straps in the rural heartland of northern Israel. By his early thirties, Republican Jesus had become an aspiring religious reformer with a clear set of positions: the poor are already blessed, weapons protect people from weapons, free health care comes only in the form of miracles, and there's no sense in saving the earth, since God will destroy it soon anyway. Most of all, Republican Jesus opposed Big Government with all of its taxes and regulations. This struggle against Big Government ended in his crucifixion—a great irony since Republican Jesus was prolife but not opposed to capital punishment.[9]

Republican Jesus is, in effect, a Protestant neoliberal capitalist in favor of small government. Keddie's description of how Republican Jesus was formed can be helpful:

From Protestantism, the Republican Jesus received his antiauthoritarian, populist attitude and his interest in saving individuals instead of classes, communities, or all humankind. He even received a less typical feature of Protestant theology in the form of the Arminian belief that a human's free will is able to overcome great adversity. This brand of Protestant theology was in many ways bestowed on the Republican Jesus through the mediation of classical liberalism.

From classical liberalism, the Republican Jesus received his affection for Small Government and his habit of protecting individual rights to property and prosperity. He also inherited a talent for lining the pockets of aristocrats and their power-hungry corporations behind the mask of protecting free enterprise.

Together, Protestantism and classical liberalism were instrumental in colonialism and the development of capitalism.[10]

Big government's rise in the progressive era created the opportunity for the Republican Jesus to be given birth among corporate elites who needed a Jesus who fit their schemes.

In my book *The Blue Parakeet*, I (Scot) relate my experience of teaching a Jesus of Nazareth class and how I came across a questionnaire given to public school students in the United Kingdom. It asked about one's own character and practices (Am I nervous? Have I ever stolen anything?). Then, after a set of questions each person answered about themselves (age, gender/sex, and the like), it asked those same questions about the character and practices of Jesus (Was Jesus nervous? Did Jesus ever steal anything?). At the end of the questionnaire, students then compared their answers about themselves to their answers about Jesus to see how much they are like Jesus! Surprisingly, most people who took the questionnaire scored a high correlation between Jesus and themselves.

This would be great—if we could be sure the answers about Jesus were completely accurate. But therein lies the problem: *everyone thinks Jesus is like them!* If a person is a Republican or a Democrat, there is a good chance they think Jesus would have been one too. Everybody thinks Jesus is on their team, so *they make Jesus like themselves*. This is exactly what Tony Keddie illustrates with his biting description of Republican Jesus.[11] Making Jesus like yourself is pure, unadulterated, and damnable—yes, damnable—idolatry. It makes God snort fire.

Our hope in this chapter is to simply draw your attention to an unfolding crisis—a crisis of witness, largely affecting Gen Xers and Millennials. Many feel they have lost their guides. Their sages have become ideologues. Those who were once lighthouses for weathering the storms of life have become cautionary, dimmed lights. Or, shifting imagery, they have been drawn in by the siren song and are now ships shattered on the rocks of ideology and tribalism. Where do we look for guidance? Young believers today no longer trust the judgment of those who were instrumental in forming their faith.

When church leaders look to leaders like Donald Trump or Jerry Falwell Jr. for guidance, is it any surprise that trust is eroded? We know people vote, and we know people choose a party to vote for. I (Scot) am old enough to have observed the evangelical alliance with the GOP for decades now, and I can think of nothing good that has benefited the evangelical movement from this alliance. Evangelicalism operates best outside the halls of power in Washington, D.C. And because we have not learned this lesson, we are now seeing the negative fruit of that alliance.

While it is not true for everyone who is deconstructing, many of those we spoke with have walked away from the faith they inherited to avoid becoming part of the problem. For them, their deconstruction is rooted in the erosion of trust, thus leading them to look elsewhere. They do not wish to hurt the church, but they must protect themselves. Having seen the trajectory of the path the evangelical movement is on, they are having second thoughts. For them, deconstruction is an act of self-preservation.

And so they are on a journey to find those who have finished well, those who went to the grave with their integrity and witness intact, those who were not seduced by power, control, or influence. Some have decided they must blaze the trail for themselves. They recall the words of a Gen X prophet, Ben Folds, in a song about losing his father: "Fresh white snow for miles, every footstep will be mine."[12] They leave footprints in the snow in hopes that their children will follow them toward Jesus. They hope to become something that has been lost—an elder generation that can be trusted and followed.

Deconstructing toward the Good

The work of the Holy Spirit is always leading Christians toward goodness, loveliness, and togetherness. When God works through the Spirit in the life of a Christian, it is always toward these things. But we often hear words of fear when people encounter those who are deconstructing and asking difficult questions. Those sitting in the pews next to them worry they are headed toward the darkness and rebellion of *the world*.

And yet in the time we've spent with deconstructors over the years, we typically do not find them to have nefarious intentions. Talking with skeptics and doubters, we often witness the opposite. A simple search query about deconstruction (especially on social media) will reveal swaths of people rethinking their faith, but they aren't there because they want to become more hateful, bitter, and rude. They aren't ditching Christianity to become more racist or judgmental or antagonistic toward others. These are the problems they are trying to escape by *leaving* the church.

As the Spirit of God within them has awakened them to injustice (both racial and economic) and ostracism (LGBTQ+ Christians, immigrants, the poor, political enemies, and the like), that same Spirit has stirred their hearts to leave. It is the same Spirit that inspired John the Baptist to call people *out* of the holy city and cross the Jordan once more to be baptized and start over again (John 3:23).

If you have not done so, we would challenge you to ask the deconstructor in your life why they left the church. It is likely to be some version of "I realized it wasn't a loving place," or "I began to see how harmful my faith was to myself and others," or even "I didn't like the way the church treated [insert marginalized group here]." Many have become aware that the harmful ideas they were trying to purge from their life were learned in the church. They realized they had embraced a belief system and a reading of the Bible that allowed these types of harmful and abusive beliefs to exist and even flourish. And they will likely tell you how they have become more loving, more accepting, and more peaceful with their neighbors since leaving. · · · · · · · · · ·

ⓢ Study — Jul 20

Deconstruction for me has been a slow process of untangling things that I grew up with/were taught in the church that hurt people around me.

The more I encounter Jesus, the more I see the toxicity and hate in the words/thoughts.

Nones and Dones

We have met hundreds of people who have—without using the terms—told us they are a Done or a None. But nearly every one of them has also told us they still love Jesus and consider themselves a follower of Jesus. More than a decade ago, Dan Kimball, a pastor in Santa Cruz, California, wrote a book with a title that is eerily true again today—*They Like Jesus but Not the Church*. What Dan pointed out then is happening today in greater numbers. People left the church because it was not "Jesus enough." It was not a place where they encountered Jesus, but was a place of empty religion. Jesus was invisible, and Dan challenged churches to rediscover Jesus, the great I Am.

Could the Nones and Dones of today help believers *re*-construct the Christian faith, not by rejecting the historic faith, but by gazing at and following the man at the center of our faith, the one who made these extraordinary claims about himself? Is it possible to begin afresh, to form a Jesus community? Is it possible to turn our backs on the religion of cultural Christianity and rediscover a "Jesus is the I Am" faith?

We believe it's not only possible—it's necessary. And we are encouraged that some of those who have left the church are turning back to the Bible to have a fresh encounter with Jesus. A longtime reader of Scot's blog who has been on her own journey of deconstruction recently wrote this:

> In my fifteen-year journey of deconstruction out of institutional church settings into being a "Done," through rubble clearing I have finally moved into a profound period of reconstruction and reorientation. It has been a challenging

yet worthy endeavor, and I am much the better for all of it—painful as it has been.

Part of the challenge during this time has been the deep need to step away from any and all traditional forms of Bible study—into a deep listening stage for the still, small voice of the Holy Spirit. Having been a joyful student of the Scriptures—First and Second Testaments—for literally as long as I have been able to read (sixty years) . . . there was plenty of Scripture buried deep in my heart that the Spirit could access. I was weary of the translation and interpretation wars of varying agendas, but especially those targeting the value and place of the sisters in kingdom family and ministry.

But I asked the Spirit today whether it was time to reengage with Scripture with eyes that have significant distance from decades of familiarity . . . and I believe I heard a strong yes.[13]

Notice that in her journey she is turning back to the Bible, to the Jesus who claimed to be the great I Am. Deconstructors know Jesus made amazing claims. But they also know that if he made these claims, and these claims are true—which they are—then the church's silencing of Jesus is wrong. • • • • • • • • • •

Ⓩ Zach – June 2023

The vast majority of people walking away from church in America are not rejecting the person and work of Jesus. They are rejecting erroneous biblical interpretations which lead to bigotry, oppression, and marginalization. This rejection isn't unchristian. It is Christlike.

Christians today may not think much of a man saying, "I Am." But first-century listeners would not have skipped by those words. They may have said, "What in the world?" while wondering to themselves, *Who does this guy think he is?* The problem we face today is that far too many believers skip past the audacious and amazing claims and teachings of Jesus. Christianity has become a religion with an institution (church) and a national culture.

If we are willing to listen, the deconstructionists of today are saying, "I want this Jesus. I want him to be front and center. I don't want religion. I don't want an institution. I want a community centered on listening to Jesus and living like him during the week." When they read of Jesus' claim to be the I Am, they mutter, *That's what I'm talkin' about!* In their deconstructing, they are not motivated to leave the church; they are looking for a community built around a reconstructed faith that exalts Jesus as Lord of all.

If church leaders are willing to listen, this is what their exit interview will reveal.

Jesus Drama

We close this chapter by challenging you to read these words about Jesus:

> Jesus, knowing all that was going to happen to him, went out and asked them, "Who is it you want?"
> "Jesus of Nazareth," they replied.
> "I Am," Jesus said.
> (And Judas the traitor was standing there with them.)
> When Jesus said, "I Am," they drew back and fell to the ground. (John 18:4–6, our translation)

Why did men of power draw back and fall to the ground when Jesus proclaimed "I Am" in Gethsemane? These men were the spiritual leaders of the Jewish community. They were by no means vanguards, but they held the hearts and faith of the Jewish people in their hands. They were connected to the holy temple, and their entire lives were dedicated to observance of the Jewish way of life.

But when they came into contact with Jesus their power shrank, shriveling away. Rarely do we think of the power of God as a threat to God's people, especially the spiritual leaders of his people—unless, of course, the power they wield over the people is *not* the power of God but some other power. Political power. Human power. Power to enact their own agendas and plans, not God's.

It is no secret that the church has always been filled with leaders who exercise authority over God's people through the use of tools that God would never use. Coercion, violence, money, bullying, retaliation, and flexing power and intellectual muscle can help a person climb the ladders of any institution, which makes it also true of Christian institutions, churches, parachurch organizations, universities, and seminaries. Men and women secure backroom deals to sell out, profit, and get wealthy on the backs of their congregations, hiding abuse to protect their institutions. Women and men of power seek to control the work of God, especially regarding the poor and marginalized. They have power, yes, but it is not the same power that Jesus possesses. In fact, the power they wield is often antithetical to the power of Jesus.

Forget all you know about Jesus' divinity and incarnation and take an objective look at Jesus' ministry. He doesn't have any credentials. He doesn't fit in any of the popular schools of Jewish thought. His students are dropouts, fishermen, tax collectors, a rabble of misfits—just poor young men and women. He isn't wealthy. He isn't royalty. He doesn't even have a home. He's not a CEO and has no advanced degrees; his gig lasts for three years, and then he is killed. There is no reason to draw the conclusion that Jesus is powerful in any way. And yet God is at work *in* and *through* him. Even though those coming to arrest him in the garden are superior in every earthly way, far more powerful than he is, God has not joined with them. God's power is only found in actions that reflect the cross.

On that night in Gethsemane, men came in the power and authority of the greatest emperor on earth, bearing his weapons. But when they met Jesus, they met the power of God. And when the power of God is present, the powers of earth have no choice but to draw back and fall away.

When earthly power creeps into the community of God, it stands in obvious contrast to the way of Jesus. Deconstructors can smell its stench. And this is why many have turned to Jesus as their defense against abuse. They love the church but are critical of un-Christlike leaders who have joined with earthly powers. They intuitively know that the power of Jesus demands humility, generosity, sacrificial love, and the willingness to give everything when love demands it.

God's power is displayed in weakness. So-called Christian leaders dabble with the power of this world like a child playing in a mud puddle while ignoring the ocean of God's power found in Jesus. But *Christlike* leaders understand that God only chooses to work through the cross-shaped acts of Jesus, not through the sword-shaped acts of a CEO, political leader, or military general.

Jesus fed thousands, walked on water, engaged in debates

with Jewish leaders, and was sought out and taken into custody, and when people wanted to know who he was, he simply said, "I Am." Full stop. Mic drop.

So, who is this man? Who does he think he is? Is he right? And if he is, what does that mean for Christians? Deconstructors, as they close the door on their way out of the church, are turning back to say, "If Jesus is the great I Am, I'm gonna go find the place where he really is the great I Am."

5 Placing Jesus in the Center

In the past, we've believed and at times dogmatically defended doctrines taught to us by parents, pastors, and professors. We've done this as if those dogmas were what mattered most about Christianity. Between the two of us, we've variously believed the rapture had to occur before 1988 and that only Republicans were Christians. We believed in six-day creationism and denounced evolution. We believed only men were allowed to be pastors. We believed the modern state of Israel could do no wrong. We believed in the penal substitution theory of the atonement to the exclusion of any other understanding of the atonement. We believed the four spiritual laws were the gospel. We believed the folks in our tribe were the only ones truly saved, though we were open to thinking there was a small number of mixed-up but still somehow Christian folks in other denominations. We believed we had to evangelize every soul we met, and we saw persons as souls, not bodies. We believed in the King James Version of the

Bible and only the KJV. We believed speaking in tongues might be, or perhaps really was, demonic, while some we knew (Scot's grandma, for example) believed just the opposite—that if you had not spoken in tongues, you had not received the Holy Spirit (and might not even be a Christian).

Some have walked away from the faith because of the pain caused by these dogmas and the demands they make. Some are triggered and begin to shake as they recall manipulations staged by leaders to create audience-impressing works of God. Both of us grew up Baptist. Perhaps that explains a lot of this.

Doctrines and dogmas. What happens to the person who begins to think the dogmas they once were taught and believed are not only wrong but, to use a sanctified word, *rubbish*? What happens when what you once believed was essential, salvific-level truth now appears in your conscience at the level of the "very seriously mistaken"? What happens when you begin to believe the penal substitution theory of the atonement might be a form of exacting revenge or, at the very least, a balancing of justice with deserts, and that it surely doesn't sound like grace or forgiveness? When what you believed was perceived by many to be part of the gospel itself but really isn't? When you've blown through that boundary marker that symbolized your faithfulness like a stop sign on a barren country road? What lies beyond the stop sign? Is it a car crash—or is it freedom? Let's start with an example.

Women, Especially Single

One of the most precious, bounded-set doctrines for many in the evangelical world goes by several different terms (depending on how irritated you might be): traditional, biblical, complementarian, patriarchal, hierarchical, masculinist, and misogynist. Whole denominations have glued bold affirmations to their doctrinal statements in bright red uppercase letters affirming complementarianism. It's a perfect example of bounded-set thinking.

In 2023, The Southern Baptist Convention violated their own principle (doctrine) of the freedom of a local church by requiring each church in their convention to agree not to call any woman on a church staff "pastor," even if that woman was pastoring people. Biblically, pastoring is not reducible to or determined by a title but by what a person does. Deconstructors googled the convention and talked about it all over Twitter. It was heartbreaking for them, but far more for women gifted by the Holy Spirit to pastor others. Bounded-set thinking often excludes women from their gifting.

It's no secret we are both irritated by this bounded set. The Bible contains examples of women teaching, prophesying, praying, and leading. Most women Bible readers notice the stories of Miriam, Deborah, and Huldah. Most know the importance of Mary, the mother of Jesus. They know about the daughters of Philip who prophesied, and they have now learned about Phoebe, Junia, and Priscilla.

They understand what Galatians 3:28 makes clear: "There is no longer Jew or Greek, there is no longer slave or free, there is no longer male and female; for all of you are one in Christ Jesus" (NRSV). It only takes a moment's pondering to realize "no longer" means a long, long time. Like forever and ever, amen. That kind of equality and giftedness runs right through the Bible—and women know this. Deconstructors know it too. And yet some continue to draw deep ditches in the sand around their beliefs.

Much of the recent tightening up among evangelicals who are emphatic about silencing women's voices in leadership arose in the wake of the Equal Rights Amendment. Complementarianism is relatively new as a movement, not even as old as *Lassie* or *Ozzie and Harriet*. While women in those shows had some traditional roles, complementarianism in the 1990s formed even stronger stereotypes. You only have to watch the Netflix documentary *Shiny Happy People* to understand what we mean. Amiright? Amen? And along with the biblical and cultural problems, there is what we refer to as the gifting problem. Some women have got the gift, and they struggle to find a place where they can safely exercise it, while there are men who do not have the gift, and they *don't* struggle to find their place. This is textbook exclusivity.

Over the past three decades, evangelicals have formed a view of sexuality, especially for single women, that has squelched the Holy Spirit, damaged the church, and harmed the church's witness. Scholar Katie Gaddini wrote a stunningly important book about single women in the church called *The Struggle to Stay: Why Single Evangelical Women Are Leaving the Church*, in which she shares her own story. Growing up in the home of an evangelical pastor, she writes, "In my mid-twenties I made a slow and deliberate walk out the door of evangelicalism and toward a life that promised more freedom. I lost my religion gradually, piece by piece, as disillusionment unspooled a tightly wound coil of belief. Until I was gone. The years I spent exiting evangelicalism were painful and riddled with family strife, broken friendships, and all-consuming fear. Simultaneously, I felt exhilarated with the thrill of my newfound liberty."[1]

Gaddini maps the stories of women who find community in evangelical churches. She shares how they grow, mature, and develop hopes for equality and egalitarian relationships. Along the way, they learn the oddities and expectations for the sexual behaviors of women, and how single women are held to the highest standards. Eventually, they discover that the men are running the house, and they become disillusioned. Some walk away from the faith, but others stay and yet remain discouraged. Here is one story Gaddini tells:

> What I found really frustrating when I joined the church at twenty-six and was identified as an all-star with heaps of potential, was that time and time again I would see men join the church at the same level and get put straight in with the church leaders. They would be taken to football games, flown over to Napa on a private plane to go to a winery. They would be supported, you know? One of the male church leaders started doing all these leadership weekends where he would take fifteen men away to a cabin in the woods and really invest in them. And nothing like that was happening for women.

Expectations and public affirmations of equality and support for the leadership of women often wouldn't materialize for these women, especially single women. Gaddini observes that "the women most likely to leave [the church] are those who feel discriminated against for their agenda, for their sexuality, or for being single and having career ambitions." What was driving these disillusioned hopes? Gaddini concludes it was "the *fervor* of the beliefs behind the concept that threatens patriarchal gender orders and provokes reprisals." What keeps single women in the church is the hope of social equality and church transformation, the hope of women arising to the level of the Spirit-given giftedness, and the hope of men growing to have genuine equal, affirming, safe relationships with women, especially single women. Many stay "expectantly waiting for a future that may never come." But some decide they've had enough, and "then, disillusioned, unraveled, and wounded, they leave."

Dogmas like complementarianism, which many women experience as patriarchy, masculinism, and even misogyny, have led women out the door of the church. They begin to wonder if male leaders think God is called Father because God, like them, is male. What philosopher and theologian Mary Daly said many years ago still rings true: "If God is male, then male is God."[2]

Many women are now coming to terms with messed-up dogmas about sexuality, which were bound tighter than a medieval corset to their Christian faith. They are prime candidates for disillusionment, doubt, deconstruction, and at times, sadly, denial of the faith. My (Tommy) wife recently reminded me of how she was dragged before the dean of women at our small fundamentalist Bible college after we were caught holding hands on a date. The dean handed her a copy of Joshua Harris's book *I Kissed Dating Goodbye* and told her, "This is our standard of dating here."

Harris, whose book is now famous as an icon of the purity culture movement, announced in 2019 that he had divorced his wife and renounced his former Christian faith.[3] Several years later, Shannon, his former wife, composed a beautiful book of self-discovery (titled *The Woman They Wanted: Shattering the Illusion of the Good Christian Wife*), recounting her own break with the faith and how her faith and sexuality were strapped together.

Many of the women who left were never interviewed or asked why they exited their church. Instead, they told their stories on blogs and websites, on YouTube and Substack, and some have written books detailing their stories. More than a few women scholars have used their professional skills as historians to tell this story, including important books by Kristin Kobes Du Mez (*Jesus and John Wayne*), Beth Allison Barr (*The Making of Biblical Womanhood*), and the eye-opening book by Valerie Hobbs (*No Love in War*). The vitriol with which they have at times been treated unmasks the misogyny and masculinism of men making decisions behind closed doors without discernment of the Holy Spirit and for whom authority and control matter more than the agenda of Jesus. This is bounded-set, exclusivist thinking all the way down, all in the name of God.

Doctrines that start out as good ideas can all too easily become rigid dogma, and this is one reason so many denominations exist. Every denomination has shaped the faith with an exclusivist approach to the Christian faith (tweet that!). What distinguished a Baptist from a Methodist was where they differed (bounded set), not where they were alike (centered set). They both love Jesus, or at least they did at the start. Deconstructors today are tired of this exclusivist approach and want an inclusivist approach where Jesus, the living, breathing Galilean, is the center. They believe that when Jesus is at the center, he draws all to himself and unites all who come to him.

What Good Is Dogma without Jesus?

I (Scot) have examined many of the stories of people who have walked away from the faith. Theologians call this departure "apostasy." After reading hundreds of stories, I've listened and learned that people leave the faith for many reasons: a perceived conflict between science and the Bible, the belief that the Bible teaches an eternal conscious torment in hell for seemingly most of the people who have ever lived, what the Bible teaches about war and violence, concerns about how Christians and pastors behave. One reason they don't leave is Jesus.

What I've learned is that many of those who end up leaving came suddenly into the faith or grew up into a faith where Jesus is little more than an agent—someone who made it all happen long, long ago but is invisible as a human being. They never see him as someone who lived and walked the sandy shorelines of Galilee. They have a faith that is pragmatic but diminishes the personal and the historical. Yet absent the one and only person who matters most in the Christian faith, faith cannot do what it is designed to do. Without Jesus, it cannot liberate human beings from sin, sickness, and systemic evil into lives of goodness and justice. If there is no person of Jesus, faith is nothing but impersonal religion.

In the Gospels, Jesus turned a few bits of bread and fish into basketfuls of both, and then he walked on water. That's a pretty good one-two punch, and it certainly drew people's attention. So he followed it up with a speech in which, more than once, he claimed for all to hear, "I am the bread of life." Saying this about himself got under the skin of some leaders, as it should have, and especially since he said it (and plenty more too) in the synagogue in Capernaum.

Even his disciples had a hard time with his teaching. Part of their problem was that the leaders in the community thought Jesus had stepped over the line, and the other part of the problem was that maybe Jesus *was* over the line. John's Gospel says some of the disciples walked away from Jesus that day. (Sorry, not some; John says *many* walked away.)

Jesus then turned to those who remained and offered them an opportunity to come forward, to take a stand. "You do not want to leave too, do you?" Note how Simon Peter answers him:

"Lord, to whom shall we go? You have the words of eternal life. We have come to believe and to know that you are the Holy One of God."[4]

Exactly! To *whom* shall we go? Notice Peter did not say, "Well, we could still believe in your kingdom and justification and all sorts of good things if we walk away." Peter's response puts *Jesus the person* in the middle of the centered set. He understood—it was all about Jesus.

I remember reading about Charles Templeton, who earlier in his life had been a famous evangelist but had walked away from the faith. Near the end of his life, he was interviewed by Lee Strobel, who asked this question: "So how do you assess this Jesus?" The man's voice softened, and he began to share how much he adored Jesus. After a few moments, the man paused. Strobel recounted what happened: "That's when Templeton uttered the words I never expected to hear from him. 'And if I may put it this way,' he said as his voice began to crack, '*I . . . miss . . . him!*'"[5] Why do you think he missed him? Because at the heart of faith, the center of the centered set, is the *only one who matters*. His name is Jesus, and sometimes Christianity and religious practice can get so far from Jesus. This is something many deconstructors understand.

The essential summons of the Bible is a call to faith—to believe and to trust; it is not to know with certainty. Trust characterizes a relationship between one person and another. The reason the Bible calls its readers to trust is that God is a personal God, and trust is essential to intimate personal relationships. Trusting Jesus means throwing your lot in the direction of Jesus and following him.

The Bible's summons to trust is *profoundly personal*. It's all about you and me and God and Jesus and the Holy Spirit. It's about you and me together. It's not primarily a matter of thinking or pondering ideas until we've formed a purity culture of thoughts that we can lock down tight. It's personal because life is personal and Christianity is personal—it's you and Jesus all the way down. And if it's not personal all the way down, it's not the Jesus faith.

Christianity stands or falls on Jesus—who he is, what he said, and what he did. It does not stand on denominational doctrines. It does not stand on complementarianism (though we have heard more than one man say, "Complementarianism is the gospel," meaning that it reflected the whole gospel . . . God help us!). It does not stand on your favorite translation, the best preacher you've ever heard, or the best articulation of the creeds. Nope. The center of the centered set is Jesus. And when he isn't the center, the whole thing implodes and falls apart.

Many deconstructors we talk with are like the Greeks of John 12, who came to Jerusalem for a high holiday. In the city, they heard about a Galilean man named Jesus, and they found one of his followers, Philip. "'Sir,' they said, 'we would like to see Jesus.'"[6] If church leaders would conduct exit interviews with deconstructors who are quietly leaving their churches, a good number of them would share about their deep disillusionment. They might say, "Sir, we thought we'd find Jesus here. But if he is here, we can't see him. We think he has left the house. So we're leaving to see if we might find out where he went."

Mine [my deconstruction] occurred when the leaders of my church, who set themselves up as God's mouthpiece, consistently and blatantly went against their very own teachings that I had been listening to for 30 years, including outright lies. It made me question everything they had ever taught me. That led me to questioning every view I held on everything. I considered walking away from Christianity forever but I chose not to. A story for another time. I apparently deconstructed in an unclassical sense since I held the Bible as my standard (???) and still ended up here *gestures wildly to this Twitter account.*

Ⓜ **Meg — Jul 20**

Denominations in Decline

You don't have to read many statistical studies of the American church to know that denominations, like leisure suits, are fading into the back corner of the demographic closet. And they are likely to stay there just in case they come back into style. Let's hope not! Before World War II, 73 percent of Americans were members of a church. Today that number is less than 47 percent.[7] Protestants and Catholics are both on the decline, with no sign of a recovery. The Nones and Dones (and Nonverts) are on the rise, none of which bodes well for churches. Ryan Burge, one of America's finest experts on religious trends, put it this way in a recent article in *Christianity Today*, American's flagship magazine for evangelicalism:

> Religious demography is a zero-sum game. If one group grows larger that means that other groups must be shrinking in size.

So that rise in the nones is bad news for churches, pretty much across traditions. When you sort Christians by denomination, mainline Protestants are continuing to show significant decline.[8]

Burge's conclusions about the mainline might still draw a few loud claps and hip, hip, hoorays in praise of evangelicals, but don't be hasty; he's not done:

By their own membership tallies, mainline denominations are showing drops of 15 percent, 25 percent, and even 40 percent over the span of the last decade. *There is little room for triumph on the evangelical side; their numbers are slipping too.*[9]

So while it is true that mainliners have gone from about 30 percent of the population to 11 percent since 1975, and evangelicals saw a rise from 17 percent in 1975 to 30 percent in 1993, the current trends are showing decline across the board. Evangelicals are now showing a decline from 30 percent down to 22 percent.[10]

Consider, for example, what's happened to the mainline Presbyterian Church (USA). Again, from Ryan Burge:

In 1984, the PCUSA reported 3.1 million members on its rolls. *The denomination has never posted a growth in membership since its inception nearly four decades ago.* It took until 1987 for membership to dip below 3 million. By 2001, there were less than 2.5 million members. A decade later, the PCUSA was down another half million to 1.95M.

According to the most recently released data from 2022,

there are 1.14 million members of the PCUSA. *That's a 63 percent decline over a period of thirty-eight years.* The denomination will be less than a million members in the next five years.[11]

Many of those who have left these denominations and their doctrines have become Nones and Dones. That is, they are no longer affiliated with a church denomination. And complaints about denominations are legion. Some are spot-on; some aren't. The larger the denomination, the more encrusted the hierarchy, the more difficult it is to change, and the more challenging it is to rise to the level of actually having one's voice be heard. Those with more niche or particular dogmas tend to generate bounded-set and exclusivist thinking.

Dogmas as Stumbling Blocks

We mention niche dogmas—dogmas about matters such as creationism and eschatology, usually derived from hyperliteral readings of the text—as *stumbling blocks* because these beliefs often lead people to stumble on the path to knowing and following Jesus. Stumbling block is the English translation of the Greek word *proskomma* used by Paul in Romans 14:13, where his goal is to quash division in the church. Paul says that when we judge each other's faith—or, to tie this in with the message of this book, when we judge each other's motives for deconstruction—we put an obstacle in the path of the pilgrim. The word *proskomma* refers to a foot striking a stone.

A stumbling stone is a term you might use when your toe bumps something, causing you to fall and maybe end your journey right then and there. Niche dogmas, which are not directly related to Jesus in an inclusivist, centered-set faith, can cause believers to trip and fall on the path of following Jesus.

There are many dangerous objects that Christians who experience discouragement, disillusionment, or discrimination may encounter on their path as they move toward Jesus. It may be someone saying that to follow Jesus requires them to accept a particular view of the cosmos, perhaps one that is at odds with observable science. Or it may be a demand to value one nation over others or choose one political party over another. It may be an experience of shame where young and old believers are made to feel guilty if they don't read their Bible every day or have a standard amount of time spent in silent prayer—or if they don't use a specific order of praise, requests, and thanksgiving.

There is no reason to make a particular form of Bible reading or prayer an obligation for following Jesus. Some people take an hour or two to wake up and don't want to read or pray first thing in the morning. Maybe they want to veg as they slowly sip a cup of coffee. Where did Jesus say that everyone has to get up at 5:30 a.m., read the Bible for thirty minutes, and pray for a solid fifteen (no cheating) before they can get on with their day? Certainly no one who has little kids. Or anyone who is a night owl.

These kinds of rules, prescribed practices, and doctrines are stumbling blocks for pilgrims who want to know Jesus. And in some cases, they are felled trees across the road—roadblocks that cause the pilgrim to halt the journey and turn around—like telling a Jesus seeker that everything from tattoos to drinking a beer is a sign they aren't right with Jesus.

Olivia Jackson, who served as a missionary in the UK and overseas, shares this story about herself:

When I was in my 20s, an ongoing back complaint flared up. I was overseas, so someone took me to a doctor they knew through the church. She was a qualified medical doctor, so her diagnosis was unexpected: I had one leg longer than the other, *which is a sign of spiritual oppression.* The remedy would be deliverance ministry.[12]

Did you catch that? This lands somewhere near the border between nonsensical or laughable and the overtly dangerous. Consider what happens to the person who experiences such a diagnosis and then does not experience (I would assume) healing but ends up (again I assume) disbelieving the diagnosis and remedy?

For some, the result is deconstructing in the face of such mindboggling experiences. Later in her book, Jackson sketches how charismatic types talk about healing, assuming all the while that God will break through with a miracle: "Churches too often offer either a toxic positivity in place of genuine wrestling with reality, labelling it 'hope,' or place blame on those who suffer, or try to use it as a 'teachable moment.'"[13] Deconstructors know firsthand that many well-intentioned teachings fall short of experienced realities.

With pastoral confidence, we can say that demands like these types of views of healing are stumbling blocks, basically ensuring the journey toward Jesus will be even more difficult. Adhering to a bounded-set approach to faith or belonging to a denomination or a local church has often been promoted in place of a call to follow the one true center—Jesus. Many have come to recognize that entire Christian organizations, churches, seminaries, and parachurch organizations (seemingly) *never intend to draw toward the center and become Christlike* and, in fact, were not created to do so. And many deconstructors are tripping over these exclusivist stumbling blocks.

Over the past few years, I (Scot) have spent gobs of time pondering two particular church models: (1) the independent, autonomous (at times, megachurch) system in which the pastor and the council are in charge of everything, though they don't usually admit it, and (2) the denominational model in which history and tradition often form a massive and nearly unchangeable institutional system. What I've observed is that both of these models *are full of stumbling blocks* for a person with a Spirit-shaped vision for change, shift, or transformation. Just try suggesting a change to the liturgy or the length of a Sunday morning service or emphasizing the importance of social justice or the need to lament over systemic racism. Just try correcting the Sunday morning preacher's sermon. Just try saying you're not so sure about inerrancy, the flood, an eternal conscious punishment in hell, or that you don't like the ESV or NIV or whatever translation happens to be in the pew racks.

Dogmas or Discernments?

Four times in one (long) dip-and-dive passage about marriage, celibacy, and divorce, Paul distinguished his teachings from the Lord's words. You can find that passage in 1 Corinthians 7. At times Paul repeated what Jesus taught, at other times he added to what Jesus taught, and at still other times he made it clear he was on his own. But at no point did he disagree with what Jesus taught. He wrote, "I say" in verse 8, and once we've read verses 10, 12, and 25 as well, we realize his "I say" implies "but not the Lord."

Paul clearly knows some of the teachings of Jesus on marriage, divorce, and celibacy preserved for us in Matthew 5:31–32 and 19:1–12. Jesus taught the permanence of the marriage covenant, the permissibility of divorce in the case of sexual immorality by one partner, and the possibility of celibacy ("eunuchs for the sake of the kingdom").

Not only did Paul distinguish Jesus' words from his own, but he also divulged that (at least) some of what he offers in 1 Corinthians 7 is his opinion. Notice that since he can't appeal to a direct order from the Lord, he offers to his readers a considered conclusion (verses 25 and 40). So what happens to our reading of this chapter when we think deeply about it as being filled with Paul's discernments and advice rather than with the direct commands of almighty God?

Keep in mind that Paul encountered new situations in his mission work in Corinth. He found that some Christ followers wanted to divorce their unbelieving spouse because they were unbelievers. Some thought celibacy was for everyone, while others wondered if it was okay to marry. When Jesus spoke on a matter, Paul sided with Jesus. But when Jesus had not spoken, Paul discerned in the Spirit what was best. As he put it, "I think that I too have the Spirit of God" (1 Corinthians 7:40).

What is clear from this passage is that this is not about communal discernment. What we read here is Paul's discernment. Many who use this passage for communal discernment end up doing exactly what Paul did not do—lay down the law. Communal discernment often results in what some call a consensus, which usually means the more authoritative voices have won, and they expect everyone to go along with the consensus. In 1 Corinthians 7, Paul doesn't demand or even expect everyone to go along with him, but rather he requests they hear him out. Paul thinks he's right. But he doesn't tell the church what to do so much as give them his advice. Some would even argue he gives them the agency to decide in light of his conclusions.

At times Paul spoke on his own. And at times we are on our own too. Paul obviously did not believe that Jesus or even the Old Testament Scriptures he had at the time covered every possible topic with absolute clarity. What he taught on his own—advocating for celibacy, for example—has not been the teaching of the vast majority of Protestants. In the church's history, what Paul seems to offer in 1 Corinthians 7 is called *adiaphora*—matters of discussion and discernment that do not rise to the level of essential teachings.

Paul continues his teaching, and after a much-debated section in 1 Corinthians 11, he closes down the discussion with a humble word that all of us would do well to hear. He said if anyone wanted to be contentious about what he wrote in verses 2–15, "we don't have any such custom [about this]" (11:16 NIV; *Second Testament*).[14]

Paul clearly knew when his opinions needed to be distinguished from rock-solid gospel truths. What Jesus says is one thing; what Paul says is another. When we fail to distinguish essential, centered-set truths from adiaphora, we make everything absolutely important gospel truth. Frankly, it becomes a farce. Ordinary people know when someone is claiming gospel truth for a matter that merits little more than a personal opinion.

Stumbling Blocks

Learning to distinguish the essentials from the adiaphora is not easy. There will be differences and disagreements, but we must do the hard work of removing stumbling blocks that keep people from meeting and knowing Jesus whenever and wherever we can.

I (Tommy) have worked in a denominational church for more than two decades. The stumbling block my congregation has run into time and time again is the desire to gather around the Lord's Table in house churches and seek *God's* will for our lives together. This practice often puts us at odds with the expectation that we will align with our *denomination's* will. We've said, "It seemed good to the Holy Spirit and to us" (Acts 15:28) to make space for outsiders around the Lord's Table. But this intention was handcuffed by those in denominational seats of power two thousand miles from our neighborhood in Tampa who live in an entirely different culture.

When we discerned a decade ago that God's desire was that women would have equal power with men in our community, the denomination again became a stumbling block. And when we sought to discern through the Holy Spirit how best to integrate our LGBTQ+ sisters and brothers into the life of the church in a way that honors and respects the differences and convictions of both denomination and congregants, the denomination again became a stumbling block. Time after time, the exercise of power over other Christians became a stumbling block to many who were seeking Jesus in our midst.

And so we ask today, how can the body of Christ be led by the Spirit (as Jesus was; Matthew 4:1) if those in power have already determined where the Spirit is leading and where we should end up? How are we to wrestle with the things of God and "contend for the faith" (Jude 3) if we've already been told exactly what our faith should look like? When we apply bounded-set thinking to new situations and cultural contexts, we risk creating stumbling blocks. What we most need in these situations is centered-set thinking.

Theology doesn't always come from the ivory towers of academia or the cubicles of a denominational office. Theology can also be local, where communities learn to follow the Spirit of God together, listening to Scripture with one another, and coming to conclusions as a local community of faith that is discerning how to live in the way of Jesus right where they are. We must respect those in leadership while also engaging locally in discerning without a strict hierarchy of gatekeepers or stumbling blocks. This may mean the conclusions one church comes to may not be the same ones that the church on the other side of town comes to.

We end this chapter with a brief, edited email we received from a woman navigating how to best serve within her church. It illustrates the problem many deconstructors have with the church's stumbling blocks. For some church and denominational leaders, these stumbling blocks are dogmas that they believe deserve the full affirmation of everyone.

> This might be a long shot, but I'm in a [denominational] church that has yet to open up the offices of deacons and priests to female leadership. It's also challenging to have meaningful conversations with the leaders on deeper topics. They just blurt things out that deserve to be explored—or even at times challenged. Then they blow off what I ask about.
>
> I otherwise love the church, but I'm struggling to know how to engage them [the leaders] on topics I desperately want to discuss but feel like I'm getting blown off on. It's frustrating.
>
> I feel like I have to sit down and shut up. I'm torn between knowing how to navigate growing in my own character and

spiritual formation, serving in my church community, and stewarding the calling and longing in my heart to teach and lead others. I've always felt more comfortable working with men or mixed groups than women-only groups. "For Women Only" is not my calling.

It's tough to find a mentor or elder in my circles to help me navigate this.

The woman who wrote this is ready to walk away from her church. She's taking the first step toward deconstruction. And when she leaves, it is highly unlikely her leaders will offer her the opportunity to sit down for an exit interview.

Interlude: Deconstruction *Is* Conversion

Though many view deconstruction as a deconversion, we want to make the unusual claim that deconstruction is more a matter of *conversion*. In his highly regarded book *Understanding Religious Conversion*, Lewis Rambo pulls together a century of scholarship on conversion—not just conversion to Christianity, but the experience of conversion in general.[1] Before his book came out, many believed conversion resulted from manipulation (which is still how many skeptics view it today). However, in the 1960s, it became clear that converts were not simply passive victims of social forces or of manipulative evangelists, but were active agents in their own conversion. Rambo discovered that someone who *converts* arrives at a crossroads in life (a crisis) and decides how to respond to new information with personal, existential implications. That is, they convert.

Thus, we both have come to view deconstruction as a matter of conversion. Five points taken from Rambo's book may lead to a better understanding of deconstruction as a conversion process rather than a *de*conversion process.

First, we must understand that people always make choices in a specific context. Everyone has a context, a world in which people around them think the same things, view the world the same way, and respond in the same manner. A person interprets their own context as the *default*, and everyone outside of that is *other*. Contexts comprehensively weave together the diverse parts of someone's life in such a way that it becomes difficult to think or see outside that particular context. This means we need to know a person's context to communicate with them or even about them. And, in order to know their context, we must learn to listen to them. We will never be able to see deconstruction as a type of conversion until we have practiced that kind of listening.

> **Ⓙ Jeremy — Jul 20**
>
> It feels like breathing in fresh air.
> A chance to explore faith and scripture. It's like being born again.

Second, there is no such thing as a conversion without a crisis. Some crises are intense. It might be the death of a partner, job loss that leads to unemployment and a place in the welfare lines, or a major health diagnosis. These sudden events can have spiritual provocations. A person may come to believe that if their response doesn't meet expectations or if they behave wrongly, they will forfeit their opportunity for redemption.

For others the faith construct may entail a slower back-and-forth. That is, a faith crisis can function like a seesaw. We give weight to some ideas and understandings that anchor our faith, that keep it rooted. But over time, we pick up bits and pieces of ideas that challenge the weighty beliefs we hold dear to our hearts. Most of the time, we ignore these challenges because the new counterweights are not weighty enough to unbalance the seesaw. But if spiritual mentors, pastors, elders, or parents shut down questions and conversation by not listening or empathizing, the counterweights begin to accumulate. Something that has been slowly building may one day shift to the point that a person can no longer remain as they were.

There is another side to the *crisis* experience that needs to be acknowledged. While a faith crisis can happen on its own, one can also be manufactured. Many preachers, revivalists, and evangelists know they can manipulate a person toward a decision, which can involve threatening the hearer with fear of eternal conscious torment or the terrifying idea that one's entire family may be raptured one day and they alone will be left behind.

Even political leaders understand how to utilize fear and anxiety to stir hearts and precipitate a "conversion." This is spiritual abuse. Anyone who has been brought into the church through a manufactured crisis may eventually leave through deconstruction. When they come to meet Jesus, his beauty—compared to the hellfire and brimstone of fear-based preaching—may well lead to a faith crisis. They may question whether their previous experience was a genuine conversion, and if they decide it wasn't, they may be unsure of what to do now. In many cases, they may view their new experience of Jesus positively while rejecting their earlier church experience as a sham.

Third, this crisis experience inevitably leads to a quest. Nobody wants to remain in perpetual crisis. It's too painful. I (Tommy) see people in crisis every week. It might be a husband who came through the church doors behind his wife and three kids, his face drooping with the hopelessness that comes from watching his faith disintegrating week after week, for years. He comes because his wife's faith seems anchored and because his children have a community. But the crisis is evident on his face, and it is clearly painful.

The church's unwillingness to listen and empathize reveals serious deficiencies in our faith and the purpose of our gathering. The modern church service is not designed for listening. Sunday mornings are shaped for one-way communication where the speaker on a platform speaks and the congregation listens. And because there is no mechanism by which we can genuinely listen to each other, the skeptic easily finds a listening ear *outside* the church. Lewis Rambo and others have labeled this stage of conversion a *quest*. The person moving into conversion seeks resolution to the crisis. That is, the person is now a seeker searching for an end to their crisis. They experiment, go to websites, and enter conversations (often on social media platforms) searching for resolution to their pain.

They've got a satchel full of questions for those who will listen. They have seen too much and have accumulated far too much counterweight on the seesaw of belief to continue pretending things are okay. They will find the answers they are looking for, perhaps in the church or perhaps elsewhere. Perhaps God will meet them in the desert as he did some of the prophets in Scripture—prophets who could no longer abide the faith crisis of wayward spiritual leaders who shut their ears and eyes to those at the margins of the community.

Fourth, the quest leads to an encounter. As a person seeks answers, they have an encounter facilitated by an *advocate*. An advocate is a credible person, a genuine witness to something beyond what the person in crisis has experienced. More specifically, they are an advocate for an idea that may resolve the crisis for the seeker. This is incarnational in the sense that it involves someone who is present, someone who makes Jesus visible. Once they meet an advocate, the seeker comes to a place of decision—whether or not to *commit* to the new way of life witnessed in the advocate.

Fifth, there is a point of decision where they either walk away or make a commitment to intensify or shift their faith. After the decision is made, there is typically some form of ritual. If they've recommitted or shifted their faith, it might be a prayer, baptism, a class, or some form of initiation. If they've walked away, it might be withdrawing from their church and joining a different group. Or it might include witnessing to their former friends by sharing their story of why they left.

Our belief is that those who leave their faith or their church community are questing to cleave tighter to Jesus. The simple story of the real Jesus often precipitates a crisis that leads to a commitment in the hearts of those who hear it. They learn that Jesus was a man condemned by the authorities, though innocent. He was a man who allowed himself to be poured out and broken for the benefit of people who hated him, while revealing the oppression and violence that prop up their power. The story of Jesus is a *powerful* story that breaks existing models and sends seekers looking for another one. In the end, many deconstructors are converts to a new way of being a follower of Jesus.

7 Burying Jesus in Production

According to Olivia Jackson, one of the best chroniclers of the process, deconstruction is "an intentional examination of one's core faith and beliefs, leading to a profound change in, or even loss of, that faith." In her research, Jackson discovered that "none of us deconstructed our faith because we just wanted to sin (usually sexually) or because it's cool." Instead, deconstructors reveal a past pattern of a very serious Christian commitment, not superficial faith. "Perhaps," she adds, "because of [our] sincerity, eventually our questions just couldn't go unasked anymore."[1] Our experience indicates a level or two stronger than "perhaps."

One of the issues that sent me (Tommy) into a journey of deconstruction was the realization that our Sunday services and precious dogmas seemed to matter more than our people. We were gathering people into a space, holding up a book, and demanding that the entire room order their lives around what the book said, regardless of the particular nuances of their lives, their history, or the context they were living in. The book reigned supreme, and that book, of course, was the Bible.

To be clear, the Bible itself is not the problem. But the Bible held high in the air was not just the Bible; it was the Bible *interpreted* in such a way that the Sunday gathering had become an institution with ceremony, ritual, hierarchy, order, and structured time. The focus of this interpretation was having *everyone just sit down and listen to one person talk on and on*. What if someone had a question? Was there any opportunity for them to ask it? Yes, later in the week. What if someone had serious doubts about what was being said? Was there a place for them in our church? Rarely.

Since much of the contemporary church experience is focused on the Sunday morning service—a gathering that defines the primary way people experience church today—we turn our attention to two key elements of the Sunday service: the sermon and the music.

Sunday Is for Sermonizers

When did Sunday worship become all about the sermon? By one person? For forty-five minutes? Every Sunday, forever and amen. (Does anyone but a preacher think there will be sermons in heaven?) When did a pastor reinvent themselves as a professor giving a lecture to a class, asking them to take notes? And why is Sunday morning organized like it is?

Deconstructors ask questions like those. And also questions like these:

- Is the sermon about our learning?
- Is the best way to learn just sitting there and passively taking in information?

- Should we be listening *and* asking, being probed *and* probing back?
- What role does participation play in growing in our walk toward Jesus at the center?
- Is the passive pew sitter part of the problem?
- Why have we created a culture so shaped by the lecture hall, so customized for the passive sitter, and so acclimated to no expectation of participation? (I ask these as a professor. I know the problem myself.)
- Are we so accustomed to the Sunday-go-to-meeting culture that people would not return if a different culture began to form? Maybe not returning is what we most need. Maybe that's exactly why so many deconstructors are doing it!

Maybe the reason so many come to church on Sunday is that *they don't have to participate at all.* I (Scot) was once asked this simple question on a podcast: "Is the role of the senior pastor biblical?" Or, to put it another way, "Did our institutional culture form Christians into thinking the senior pastor is the one and only model for leading a church?"

What's the purpose of a Sunday gathering? You may say, "Worship." But where do you get that idea? Does the Bible instruct early Christians to gather in order to worship? Let's see chapter and verse. What is worship? Is it singing? One song, two songs, or three songs? Standing? Raising hands? Holding hands open?

The intent of the early church's gatherings was to nurture believers into being more and more like Christ, a goal that could be facilitated by fellowship, instruction, exhortation, correction, prayer, the Lord's Supper, praising God in song, collecting funds for the church's ministry and the poor, and living in a way that glorifies God. That's what church is all about; all of that summarized into one word, when combined with the 24/7 life, is *worship*.

But do these elements describe our church's assembling culture? Are we actually, measurably, and demonstrably nurturing believers into being more and more like Jesus? To be fair, one could answer, "Partly."

If we observe the posture of people when they gather for a Sunday service, we may conclude that our formation process tends to create passive listeners. All the chairs face the same direction (conformity) toward the preacher (spiritual authority, possessing the only voice) on the elevated stage (exalted location). Once a month (at least in some churches), we take *Communion* with a single bite of bread and a single sip of wine (the table is de-emphasized).

This was the only type of gathering I (Tommy) was familiar with as I grew up in the church, and that experience formed those who gathered. We attended and sat shoulder to shoulder as an act of submission to the person with spiritual authority, including the message they were delivering. To attend was to submit and conform.

The problem arises when you have a question about, or disagree with, what the preacher says. What do you do when they deliver a message you cannot submit to because you believe the message is unloving to your neighbor? The very act of turning away from the message and its messenger requires you to turn your shoulders so you are no longer facing forward and no longer in line with the shape of the room. To disagree is to risk alienating yourself from everything and everyone.

Is the posture of passive conformity a posture God intended Christians to take? Is this really the way Jesus would gather people? We don't think so. Sure, we recognize the need to meet in ways people find culturally comfortable. So we suggest keeping the tradition alive while *also* pointing to other ways of gathering that are less coercive, manipulative, and fear-inducing for those who dissent. These people may be few in number, but it's worth doing for any who want to participate.

Sunday Is for Entertainers

When did our Sunday gatherings become a form of entertainment, a facsimile of a concert? The musicians (I, Tommy, am one) are called worship leaders—a term that has blurred the lines between a concert and a corporate worship gathering over the last couple of decades. At one time, we saw a separation between CCM (music for Christian entertainment and encouragement) and corporate worship music—that is, music written for the purpose of being sung in communal gatherings. But in the mid-2000s, there was a collective realization among musicians in the CCM world that far more money could be made in corporate worship music. Suddenly *all* Christian music was worship music. CCM bands became worship bands overnight, and a new industry was born.

Sadly, instead of reflecting on music's role in the church and asking deep questions about how music and song lyrics form them, the churchgoer was primarily influenced to *feel* something and to *purchase* something, say, a song or an album. Now you can take the worship band *with* you. You can be *alone* in your *communal worship* singing.

Worship music became entertainment, and music as *entertainment* turns our focus inward, like pressing the button on your phone to turn the camera around so you can look at yourself. This certainly has its place, and my own spiritual journey was formed in many good ways by CCM music in all its varied forms—from contemporary, to rock, metal, and hip-hop. It all belongs. But music as a tool for *worship* should turn listeners outward toward God, the community, and the world.

Inward and Outward Music

Up until the invention of the phonograph, the vast majority of music that Christians engaged with was created as a collective outward expression of communal beliefs, theological reflection, and vision casting that took the form and feel of the local culture. From the Gregorian chants of the seventh century to Sacred Harp singing in New England in the late nineteenth century, local cultures provided the medium, the canvas, and the theology. The music they created was naturally outward facing, and it looked and sounded like those gathered geographically to worship. Think of the pain of a blues-tinged minor chord in a Black gospel song as it bends, reaching for hope. Or the invitation of a two-step Appalachian gospel song to invoke joy and togetherness. Have you felt a sense of awe as the sacred songs of the Catholic Church echo through a stone cathedral in an ancient medieval town? The songs of the church have historically been focused on drawing the Christian outward, toward our neighbor.

With the ability to record music came the ability to create music, not just for communal enjoyment, but also for artistic expression. As the role of music changed in our lives, so did the place and purpose of worship music. This is most obvious in the propensity of many churches to sing in a darkened auditorium, with the stage lit up like a Christmas tree. This de-emphasizes the crowd, and with the lights off, the diversity of cultures of those gathered is hidden and easily ignored.

The music itself is easy to digest because modern worship music is often culturally flat by design (curiously, it seems to reflect White cultural mores). It is created to appeal to as wide an audience as possible, across thousands of Christian denominations around the world, so it can never be too specific for fear that it may close potential markets. Some American churches have been known to obsess over lyrical details (remember the debate over whether or not to sing "sloppy wet kiss" or "unforeseen kiss"?), so it's best to never get too deep in the weeds about oppression, the blood of Christ, loving our enemies, or reminding people that "the body they may kill: God's truth abideth still."[2]

If, as seems to be the case today, the vast majority of churches are singing songs from just a handful of churches, we may be inadvertently making two errors: (1) promoting a form of cultural supremacy and (2) turning worship music inward toward self. Augustine, in his *Confessions*, described sin as a human being curving in on oneself (*homo incurvatus in se*). Worship music forms its listeners—there is no doubt about that—but the question is *how* it is forming listeners. From here, it doesn't look to be forming anyone toward Jesus.

Building a Church on the Wrong Mountain

In an April 2023 article titled "How Bethel and Hillsong Took Over Our Worship Sets," Bob Smietana looked at how the phenomena of big-show church formed the worship of modern faith communities. He found that almost every one of the thirty-eight most-sung worship songs in churches across the country "originated from one of four megachurches."[3] Many of these songs that magnify our poor, homeless, crucified, buried, and risen Jesus were, paradoxically, written by some of the wealthiest and most influential Christians of our day. Unsurprisingly, this is a paradox that taps into the concerns of some deconstructors. If you want to see one of these groups *live*, you can currently find Hillsong United tickets with an average price of $400. The show rivals a Taylor Swift stadium event.

Songs like these form the church, albeit poorly. The real question is whether Bethel and Hillsong songs have made listeners more Christlike. If you need evidence that they have not, read the news media about church life today. Many of the most popular songs—what we call *mountaintop* songs—make little to no reference of the crucifixion, loving enemies, dying to self, or God's resurrection power that comes through the cross. Yet these songs have become "one of the primary ways of connecting with God—rather than prayer or sacraments or other rituals. Because of their market success, these churches have changed the spiritual practices and sometimes even the theology of congregations from many traditions."[4]

These songs are mountaintop songs because the act of singing them in a church service is intended to produce an ecstatic experience. This calls to mind the scene in Luke 9 in which Jesus taught his followers about the fullness of his glory, and he did so in two steps. First, he took Peter, James, and John to the top of a mountain (traditionally thought to be Mount Tabor), where Jesus was miraculously changed and his clothes became dazzling white. The disciples saw Jesus standing between two of Israel's greatest prophets, Elijah and Moses. Of course, the disciples were excited, and Peter suggested they build huts so they could sit together out of the sun. Then the Father spoke: "A voice came from the cloud, saying, 'This is my Son, whom I have chosen; listen to him'" (Luke 9:35). Then Jesus told his disciples they couldn't remain in that beautiful place—with all the lights and smoke, the famous leaders, and the voice of God loudly affirming them.

In the second step, Jesus led the disciples to another (very different) mountain—to Mount Golgotha—where they saw him die by crucifixion between two prisoners, men without honor. The two great prophets were replaced by two criminals. Storm clouds gathered instead of a bright white mist. The beautiful white garments were stripped from Jesus, and he was left naked, clothed in shame. Instead of hearing the affirmation of the Father's love, Jesus cried out to the Father, alone and abandoned.

Where did the disciples see the full glory of God? Was it displayed for them on the mountain where Jesus was transfigured, or on Golgotha?[5] God's glory is displayed, not through the "big show," but through the "big serve"—in the service of giving one's life for others. When we plot and spend money to impress the world into believing in Jesus, we create a false portrait of Jesus. We proclaim the glory of victory instead of the good news of the cross. In this way, our worship successes become our excesses of failure.

Music is a tool for worship, but there are other elements of worship as well. Let's pause and think about worship through the Communion elements—the bread and wine. Throughout church history, the central act of worship has typically not been the sermon or the music; the main event on the church's stage has been the Lord's Table—the celebration of the wine and bread, the blood and body. The act of the participants has been to take and eat, to take and drink. It has not been an experience of ecstasy,

but rather of humility. It's not the mountaintop, but hands out-
stretched and knees bent. The bread is just flour and water; the
wine is aged grapes. These are common things that most people
at some point throughout a week would consume. But the gathering of the church is not the same. Having a slice of garlic bread
with your Pinot Noir is not the same as participating in the Lord's
Supper, just as singing a catchy song about God is not the same
as worship.

Both Communion and singing worship music require purposefully seeing Christ in that common, everyday object or
experience. It involves taking an everyday object and injecting
profound and deep meaning into the elements. It is the practice of taking part *in* them, of seeing the divine in the common
and choosing to see the work of God in the simple act of sharing
and eating, thereby creating an act of *worship*. Music is simply
sound put to time, but what it *does* to a roomful of people can
vary, depending on the focus of the leader. Music can inspire love,
unity, and even justice and protest. It can create focused anger,
joy, comfort, or any range of emotions that can help a community
grow spiritually or grieve deeply.

Again, we are left with the question of formation: Is the time
we set aside for music and singing about performers on a platform
wowing the audience, or is it about believers leading believers into
worship?

Deconstructors and the Table

A growing phenomenon, developed by those who dream of what
church could be, is gaining popularity among those who are
deconstructing their faith or turning away from the aesthetic of

Sunday morning institution—the house church, a form of small group gathering. House churches are small communities that meet in homes or other informal settings, often around a dinner table. They are less formal, more participatory, and typically have a flatter leadership in contrast to the traditional hierarchical structure of many institutional churches.

A pastor, who for many years preached on the massive platform of a megachurch, sat down with me (Scot) over coffee and made this confession (paraphrased):

> If we tossed away our weekend services, I would not miss a thing. The only "church" that matters to me is our small group. It is there that I worship, learn, pray, and experience fellowship. Sunday is because we "have to." Small group is because "I want to" and "I need to."

Curious, I asked him what they did together in his small group, and this was his reply: *We eat together at the table.*

I believe this confession has three expressions that need to be glued together: *church*, *small groups*, and *table*. That's the church. In a recent study of why Americans are dechurching, the most common reason has to do with relationships. Either they don't fit in, don't feel loved, have moved and couldn't make connections, or don't have friends at a church. The study further suggests that friendship could draw them back to church.

Though our purpose in writing this book is not to offer advice on how to win them back, we know it's a valued goal for many. Rather, we find this conclusion interesting because it supports our broader contention that *the culture and institution of churches have fallen away from their basic social capacities to establish friendships that can lead to genuine Christian fellowship.*[6] This lack of relationships reveals a deep problem in the church: the posture of passive sitting is not forming people for active participation and growth. (Tweet that.)

House churches have played a key role in gathering believers together in places like China, India, and parts of Africa for decades; according to some estimates, there are as many as 10 million house churches in China alone. It is far more difficult to gauge the size of the house church movement in the West. While there is evidence to suggest the movement is growing, house churches operate independently and are not included in institutional counts or surveys.

For many, the appeal of the house church gathering is that it exercises power differently from a traditional gathering. There is no time constraint, and the smaller size offers opportunity for discussion and disagreement. People can offer pushback against any assumptions about God, faith, and the Christian life. Instead of sitting with shoulders aligned facing a solo messenger, the gatherers' shoulders face one another in a circle, facing the image of God in others as they share their thoughts and then listen while others speak. Those present read the room and can immediately gauge whether the word spoken brings life and freedom or bondage and fear.

And there's usually food too. The table in these gatherings embodies provision—being filled up, hunger satiated; serving others; and enjoying the broken bread and poured-out wine. The faces they see are more paramount than the performance on a stage. Jesus, by his Spirit, is present to anyone and everyone. The question is no longer, *What do I need to believe in order to belong?* but rather, *Why has God brought this person to the table? How can I become a sibling to them? What does God want to say to me through them, and how can I serve them? What am I being called to be or do in this relationship?*

The Language of the Table

Jesus promised that when we gather at the table in his name, he is present. Jesus' first move was not giving us a list of doctrines to affirm before we partake. No, he invited people to the table, blessed the bread and wine, and encouraged them to eat and drink. At the table, we learn one another's names and stories, and in better knowing one another, we learn to better know the Jesus who is present with each of us. At no point does the person who brought or cooked the food become the authority in the room. At the table we are equals. We share dishes and pour drinks for one another. We clean up the table together. We make sure everyone has what they need before they depart.

Our current Christian institution of the Lord's Supper developed out of the context of ordinary meals eaten with ordinary food with ordinary people listening to Jesus and asking him ordinary questions. There were no precision-cut mini-breads, nor did they serve the wine in little plastic cups. They shared bread, unleavened at times, and drank diluted wine. Think food, sitting on the ground, and bad breath and B.O. Nothing sanitary or sanctimonious about those gatherings. In fact, much of what we mean by "ceremony" and "institution" when we talk about the table is the sanitary nature of the way it is done. Many of those in deconstruction mode have left the ceremony but still love the bread because it is given by Jesus. Those who love his bread know he's got a vision for those without bread.

At the church where I (Tommy) serve in Tampa, Florida, we have been gathering as house churches for fifteen years. We continue to gather on Sundays to take Communion and hear Scripture proclaimed, but the Sunday gatherings are no more important to us than the fourteen house churches that gather around Tampa Bay on any given weeknight. Our collective deconstruction demanded a more intimate gathering. We needed an opportunity for dissent, a way to call BS on the accessory beliefs and practices that Western culture has attached to the institutional church. And more than anything, we needed a place and time—and some freedom—to get to know, to love, and to listen to one another.

Sometimes the liturgy, or orderliness, of the church no longer gives life and becomes burdensome. The stuffiness of a religious custom is nothing new. The Sabbath is a great example of this. In Mark 2:23–28, Jesus was questioned by the religious leaders about fasting. Jesus' disciples traveled alongside him, and as they walked through a field, they picked little heads from the wheat stalks and rubbed them in their hands to separate the grains, and then ate them. It was the equivalent of eating a handful of sunflower seeds. Yet some of the religious leaders were beside themselves. "Look, why are they doing what is unlawful on the Sabbath?" (Ugh, because they were hungry.)

Then Jesus uttered a profound spiritual truth the church today has ceremoniously ignored. Jesus said, "The Sabbath was made for man, not man for the Sabbath" (Mark 2:27). Sabbath was meant to bless people—to be a day for rest and entering into refreshment. But humans have a habit of turning the gifts of God, like Sabbath, into a burden. The hungry must wait for food because an *institutional authority* says so. Yet the deconstructor replies, along with Jesus, *If your religion prevents you from feeding another person, your religion is worthless. It's good for nothing more than being thrown in a barrel and incinerated.*

The rising skepticism and subsequent deconstruction we see in the church today demands that we rethink how we gather as the people of God. The church must find ways to become flatter, less hierarchical, and less institutional. We need to be more intimate, more social, more equal, more participatory, more relational, and far more transparent. It is time to stand face-to-face or in a circle and proclaim what we know is true about our King through laments, protests, choirs, and corporate prayers. It is time to face each other in confession and admit the ways our community has created oppression. And we need to stand face-to-face with one another as we share bread and wine, because when the body allows itself to be broken and poured out, the world experiences true healing through Christ.

We want the Bread of Life himself. For everyone. For at the table, one is sustained by the Bread. And the Bread is for *the whole world*—imagine that! A professor tells a story about a student who came to their office to deconstruct her faith. She was concerned with "what Christianity was supposed to look like." More accurately, she was trying to understand "why the evangelical tradition she identified with didn't reflect the values she saw important to Jesus."[7]

Many deconstructors have lost all patience with the lack of care the church shows for the poor and hungry. How can his followers be agents who distribute his bread for the sustenance of others when they too often turn away from the hungry in their communities? Deconstructors have learned about Jesus, and they want the church, whether it's a megachurch or a house church, to take its cues from the Bread himself.

In an article titled "World Hunger Facts: What You Need to Know in 2023," Concern Worldwide shares that "2.3 billion people—29.6 percent of the world's population—don't have adequate access to food," and "828 million people go hungry every day," with more than 40 percent of this number facing "acute levels of hunger." More women than men are at risk, and more children than adults, with 149 million children experiencing stunted growth because they lack food.[8]

Food matters—and providing food matters—especially for someone who calls herself or himself a follower of Jesus. In the Bible, food matters. Provision for the poor and hungry matters. If you look in the Bible for the words *hunger, hungry,* and *poor*, you will find hundreds of occurrences. The book of Exodus contains an amazing story about God's provision of manna for the Israelites in their desert wanderings, a time when they were especially vulnerable to food shortages, hunger, and nutritional deficits (about which they barely knew anything).

The story begins with a food shortage, with people struggling with hunger and deep fears about future provision and possible starvation. The Israelites complained, "If only we had died by the LORD's hand in Egypt! There we sat around pots of meat and ate all the food we wanted, but you have brought us out into this desert to starve this entire assembly to death" (Exodus 16:3). They lamented that they'd had enough food in Egypt but were now *starving.*

In response, God promised to "rain down bread from heaven" (Exodus 16:4)—mark that expression—and Moses delivered a message from God, instructing each family to go out daily to collect enough for their family for just that day, and no more. God's provision would come one day at a time, except on the sixth day, when they could collect for two days because no work was to be done on the sacred Sabbath.

The people were not happy with a menu of manna alone, so God also gave them quail. The word *manna* sounds something like, "What is it?"—a question the children of Israel asked when they first saw it. No matter how you read the story—whether it's about grumpy people or variety on the menu—a six-days-a-week act of God provided for those in need. Because that's the kind of God Israel had.

We all wish for more miracles, but perhaps we find the miracle we need when we consider something the apostle Paul wrote on one of his many mission trips. Since he was acutely aware of the poverty of many Jesus followers in Jerusalem, he began a mission fund for the poor saints, pleading with and even guilting other believers into contributing to his fund. Here's how he explains it:

> Our desire is not that others might be relieved while you are hard pressed, but that there might be equality. At the present time your plenty will supply what they need, so that in turn their plenty will supply what you need. The goal is equality, as it is written: "The one who gathered much did not have too much, and the one who gathered little did not have too little." (2 Corinthians 8:13–15)

There are a few observations about Paul's version of the "manna miracle" we'd like to point out. First, Paul's goal is *to provide food for the poor and hungry*. Second, his goal is *equality*. What does he mean by equality, you ask? He quotes from the manna story in Exodus, reminding us that each person gathered enough for the family—no more and no less. Everyone had what they needed. That's what Paul meant by equality in the Christian sense. It didn't mean everyone received the same amount or got paid the same. But what it did mean is that everyone had what they needed—and what is needed is food, clothing, and shelter. (And, in our day, you may argue that the internet belongs with these other essentials.)

Paul believed a manna miracle opportunity had arisen for ordinary Christians in all his mission churches, and he believed God was moving them to provide manna for those in need. They were to use their abundance to meet the needs of others in their scarcity.

Deconstructors are aware of the abundance of the church and the scarcity of others. They are well acquainted with the reports of some pastors who rake in thousands upon thousands of dollars, with access to funds for their pet projects, and they know ordinary people who sacrificially donate their resources with discipline, even in the midst of financial scarcity.

Deconstructors see the disparities between what wealthy Christians have and what others don't have. They consider what we eat and what others don't eat. Not a few have pointed out to us in conversations that the meaning of the word *equality* in the passage cited above has been softened and diminished in some translations to mean something less (like "fairness" in the ESV). And who can be against fairness? Well, God, Paul, and many of us. The Greek word *isotes* means equality, and equal means, well, equal. Equal does not mean disproportionate. "Isosceles triangle" is derived from this Greek word—a triangle with two equal-length sides, not all that different from an equilateral triangle in which all three sides are the same length.

"Share with those who are in need" is the motto for Paul and Moses, and it's also the way of Jesus. It means every single body in the church and—because equality in the church becomes a virtue the church models and exhibits for the world—every single body in the whole world should get what they need.

Perhaps you're thinking this is too radical. I beg you not to think of what's radical or realistic, or even of how much poverty existed in Paul's lifetime. Think instead about God and his love for the created world, about God's image in everyone in the world, and about our abundance and whether we are using it to help others. Imagine a world in which each person had sufficient food and drink every day. That's the manna miracle called equality. Deconstructors today believe in this kind of equality, and they are becoming a prophetic voice.

So think about church, a small group, and the table. Then add the bread, as the symbol of the Bread of Life.

Bread in a Basket

One of the truly astounding acts of Jesus was his provision of bread and fish for the poor and hungry. It's an event recorded in all four Gospels.[9] Something happened that was so stunning that each of the gospel authors had to tell their own version of the event. As often happened, Jesus' closest followers were clueless. They wonder how such a large crowd could be fed so far away from any food supply. They are like many of us when it comes to the needs of our world and the part we can play in meeting those needs. What is even more mystifying is how they were again clueless when the same need arose not long afterward. It's understandable for the disciples to think Jesus couldn't pull an endless menu from his bag of miracles, but it's downright dumbfounding to lack that expectation a second time around.

Yet again, however, Jesus fed thousands by filling the basket of each of the twelve disciples. So abundant was the provision that each of the Twelve returned with a full basket. Surely this sent a message that there was enough—and more than enough—for all. Food matters. Food matters to Moses, Jesus, and Paul because they all think alike. Food matters, and whoever is in tune with God will do what they can to provide food for the hungry. As we wrote above, 828 million people experience hunger every day, a number that ought to burn its way into our hearts and liberate our checkbooks for the good of the hungry.

The *what* is not as important as the *who*. Take the crowds that experienced "Manna Miracle 2.0." Their thoughts turned beyond the physical act of multiplying food to the Miracle Worker himself: "Surely this is the Prophet who is to come into the world," they muttered among themselves (John 6:14). But Jesus saw more at work underneath their mutterings. He perceived they wanted to "make him king" (6:15). Interesting, isn't it? Instead of talking about the tastiness of the bread, they wanted to talk about Jesus. They perceived that this miracle revealed the doer of the miracle as much as the act of multiplying food itself. And that's the same point we hear from deconstructors. *Jesus*, they say, cares about more than the soul, more than the church, more than your body and mine. *Jesus* cares about the poor and the hungry and the underfed.

What does it mean to follow *the Bread of Life himself* if you don't care enough to take from your abundance and provide for those in need? Their criticisms contain a sharp barb or two, but you have to admit they ask a question that points to Jesus—the "I am the bread of life" (John 6:35). On their way out the door, if we truly listen to what they have to say, deconstructors might say they don't see Jesus in our churches and they're going to find the Bread among those who need bread.

Church, small group, table, bread of the Bread.

Or church, sermon, and band?

Bread of Life: Three Realities

When people turn to Jesus as the Bread of Life, bread itself becomes an icon pregnant with meaning, spurring imagination, and even offering some provocation. When we see Jesus as the Bread of Life, at least three realities take priority for us, three dimensions of a life worth living. Jesus identifies himself as the Bread that gives life eternal, which means more than living with God after we die; eternal life means that, both in this life and in the next, the life of God sustains and flourishes in our bodies in a way that reveals the meaning of life.

First, Jesus provides physical, material bread to physical, material bodies so those bodies can be nourished and sustained with life. Hunger ends when the body works the nutrients of food into its system. Moses cared. Paul cared. Jesus cared. And we need to care as well. We need to care about the absence of food and the ripping away of any kind of meaningful life because of hunger and poverty. Most deconstructors we talked with care deeply about poverty and hunger. They believe a church that doesn't care about hunger is not a true church.

Feeding America reported several years ago that faith-based groups represented 62 percent of its network of food banks; at the same time, according to 2018 statistics from the National Study of Congregations' Economic Practices, about *half* of faith communities were committed to food distribution in their communities.[10] And while some may look at that number as evidence that churches are helping, deconstructors are asking, "Where the hell are the other 50 percent?" (Forgive us for putting it that way, but that's what they're saying.) And if you think about it, they're right. What's wrong with our churches that *only somewhere between 50 and 60 percent of churches* are putting manna on the doorsteps of their neighbors?

Paul saw equality on the manna menu. Jesus had twelve full baskets of food left over after his provision. But where are the rest? Anyone who follows Jesus commits to distributing food to the hungry. That is, *everyone* who follows Jesus should participate in food distribution because that's just the way Jesus is. Let's commit to make *equality* our motto. There are more than twelve baskets left over in America's economic system, more than enough for all.

Second, Jesus provides life that transcends the material, embodied life. Every one of the "I am something" statements concern life. If you say, "I am," John says, "life." But when *eternal* is stuck to *life*, that word *eternal* gets jammed in the printer. Sometimes Christians preach a message and share a gospel that is all about going to heaven when we die. For them, Jesus gives eternal life because they will live with God forever. But the word *eternal* cannot be reduced to Randy Travis's twangy "forever and ever, amen."

The word *eternal* translates a Greek term that translated the Hebrew *olam*, and it means era, epoch, period. It refers to life that connects to the Jesus Era. To be sure, that era lasts forever, but—and this is a huge difference—eternal life begins now, that is, the moment one gets linked to the life Jesus is and provides. Notice that Jesus says people now can pass from death to life (John 5:24) and thus people already "have" eternal life (6:47). The I Am who is Jesus launches the Jesus Era, and the Jesus Era launches those who turn to him into eternal life, not in the future, but beginning at that very moment.

Eternal life means a life worth living. It means flourishing—you being you for the purpose for which you are designed. To quote Miroslav Volf, one of America's major theologians, along with his student Ryan McAnnally-Linz, "In other words life that goes well, is lived well, and feels as it should. In this kind of ordinary life, the powers of eternal life are already at work. The line separating abundant created life . . . and eternal life isn't sharp." For Volf and McAnnally-Linz, eternal life is a life liberated from sin and death, from the powers that are against us and oppress us (like poverty and hunger). Eternal life is more than "mere indefinite prolongation" but "an unending fullness of true life in all its dimensions."[11] And it exists in the here and now.

Third, Jesus reveals that he—not the church, not your pastor, not the institutions that burned you—is the DNA of the cosmos. To get more insight into what Jesus meant when he said "I Am," let's consider his statement, "I *am* the bread of life" (John 6:35). The Gospel of John frequently uses the word *life*, and about Jesus, John declares, "In him was life, and that life was the light of all" mankind (1:4). Those who believe in Jesus have eternal life (3:15–16), and if people drink the water Jesus provides, that water "will become *in them* a spring of water welling up to eternal life" (4:14, italics added). But this life is more than just a gift *from* Jesus; *he* is the life. John writes, "For as the Father has life in himself, so he has granted the Son also to have life in himself" (5:26). Life is at work in Jesus in such a way that his "words . . . are full of the Spirit and life" (6:63).

Deconstructors are looking for life, for the one who is the Bread that gives and provides life itself. If we see Jesus this way, we begin to see through Jesus into a brand-new life for a brand-new world—a world in which the breadbaskets will overflow for all, a world of equality. One reason deconstructors disengage is that they do not see this Jesus in the church. They do not feel the church believes in Jesus or that it embodies the dimensions of life he brings.

Many deconstructors believe the church needs to repent and turn back to Jesus, recentering on him and decentering on leaders and pastors. The church needs to rediscover what C. S. Lewis meant when he said, "I believe in Christianity as I believe that the Sun has risen, not only because I see it, but *because by it I see everything else.*"[12] Another way to say: we believe in Christianity as we believe in the Bread, not only because the Bread feeds me, but because the Bread makes us all equal.

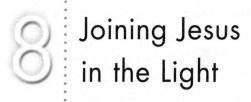

Joining Jesus in the Light

Speaking up and speaking out will earn you some critics. Some will be loud; some will be angry; some will be powerful and shove you off the platform. Sometimes deconstructors speak best by walking away. Sometimes the critic meets with church leaders who demand answers by pounding the deconstructor with a steady stream of loaded questions. Sometimes these leaders gaslight the questioner into submission. Sadly, people who have questions are not always welcome in the church. And those who advocate answers to questions that differ from the status quo can end up in a heap of tears. Here are three stories to consider.

One

For six years, Jason pastored a church made up of many young families. Some, like Jason, were going through a journey of deconstruction after growing up in a stringent expression of Christianity that didn't allow drums on the stage, let alone women. Then the letter of 1 Timothy was next up in Jason's exegetical preaching schedule—more specifically, chapter 2. On the surface, this chapter appears to contain prohibitions regarding what women can and can't do in the church. But along with these apparent prohibitions were some bizarre statements that Jason had never noticed or that had been de-emphasized in his theological training.

Jason was preparing to preach on what he at the time believed was the biblical position as found in 1 Timothy 2:11–12: "A woman should learn in quietness and full submission. I do not permit a woman to teach or to assume authority over a man." *Fair enough*, Jason thought to himself. "I've always been raised to believe," he said to me (Tommy) in a conversation we had, "that women are to serve under men in the church, though I wish things were different. But then I " verse 15: 'But women will be saved through childbearing—if they continue in faith, love and holiness with propriety.' I didn't believe for a second that these words should be taken literally—nobody did. And even though I didn't really know how else to understand this verse, I knew it didn't mean what it said on the face of it."

Confronted with problems in his own literal reading of the text, Pastor Jason suddenly didn't know what to do. He believed the text should be taken at face value, yet he did not believe that that a woman must give birth to be saved. His own sister was infertile, and her and her husband's struggle to have kids was a constant source of pain and anxiety. How could he look at two verses in the same paragraph in the Bible and take one literally but ignore the other?

And so Jason did what any good pastor should do. He began to search for a way to make sense of it all, starting with commentaries—older ones first. Most of them offered no answer other than an attempt here and there to make the verse about Mary giving birth to Jesus, an interpretation that seemed forced and desperate.

Pastor Jason committed to spend five weeks in this passage so he and his church could do a deep dive together. His studies led him to ancient writings about Artemis (Diana) and the Artemision in Ephesus; this cult worship included elaborate hairstyles and incantations. "At the end of those five weeks, I stood behind that pulpit and told the congregation that I was starting to think Paul wasn't actually silencing women everywhere, just probably some very specific women in Ephesus. I admitted to my people that I was starting to think that perhaps we were wrong, that we've misunderstood this passage, and that I feared we might be hindering the work God wanted to do through the women in our congregation. It didn't go well."

He looked at me after recounting the whole ordeal with his critics. "That was pretty much the end of my time as a pastor," he said. When last we spoke, he was working his way into management at a local Ikea store. "I've been replaced by someone who can ignore the passages people want them to ignore and emphasize the passages that keep them comfortable. They said, *You won't find itching ears here!* and they said it without a hint of irony."[1]

Two

In 2014, Michael and Lisa Gungor, the husband-and-wife duo who make up the groundbreaking worship band Gungor, were one of the most successful acts in Christian music. Their album *Beautiful Things* was released in February 2010 to critical acclaim and praise from fans, reaching number seven on the Billboard Top Christian Albums chart. Four years later, however, they found themselves in the crosshairs of critics, conservative Christian magazines, and online publications.

In an interview, Michael admitted he no longer believed in a literal reading of Genesis. The *Christian Post* picked up the story in an article published on August 5, 2014, titled "Dove-Award Winning Gungor Rattles Christian World with Revelation That They Don't Believe the Bible Literally." They capture Michael's words:

> "Over the last year, I have had so many questions asked of me about what I believe. Just tonight I had a conversation with someone extremely close to me that said that he wouldn't consider me a Christian anymore," explained Gungor in the post.
>
> "Why? Not because of my life . . . Not because my life looks like Jesus or doesn't look like Jesus. But because of my lack of ability to nail down all the words and concepts of what I exactly BELIEVE. Because I've lost so many of the unconscious assumptions that I used to have and have no ability to un-see what I have seen," he explained.
>
> "I have no more ability to believe, for example, that the first people on earth were a couple named Adam and Eve that lived 6,000 years ago. I have no ability to believe that there was a flood that covered all the highest mountains of the world only 4,000 years ago and that all of the animal species that exist today are here because they were carried on an ark and then somehow walked or flew all around the world from a mountain in the middle east after the water dried up," he continued.[2]

Those who observed this from the outside saw how things go when someone steps "out of line." Typically, such persons are presented with an ultimatum: "Believe in that which does not make logical sense or give up everything you have worked and lived for." People can move on to another career path, but they cannot live well if they lose their integrity. Deconstructors have learned the difficult lesson that exercising one's intellectual integrity in the church often means the *loss* of their church, ministry, pastorate, or career. In these scenarios, having a lack of integrity is actually an advantage when it comes to doing your pastoral work.

Gungor's songs were subsequently pulled from radio stations, and a growing base of critics started denouncing the couple, often interrupting Q and A sessions to ask antagonistic questions and writing slanderous online articles. There was almost no effort to have a rational conversation about science, the book of Genesis, or the interpretation of ancient texts. This was ideology on full display. It had become clear to critics that Gungor had stepped out of line, and those in the seats of power no longer had any use for them. They also found out rather quickly they no longer had a place in the church. With no place to ask their questions, they set out on a pilgrimage that led them and hundreds of thousands of listeners to their top-rated podcast, *The Liturgists*. They landed in a wilderness of wandering and searching, of deconstruction and agnosticism, in a home we might call "Not Knowing." But it didn't have to be that way.

Many of us watched these unfolding events intently because *we* have had similar thoughts. We have been asked to ignore what was obvious in exchange for something that was obviously false, and we understand what happens when you do not play along. Seeing what happened to Gungor didn't put the fear of God in us; it put a fear of *the institution* in us. The critics were winning. That was the year many of us learned to keep our mouths shut. We learned to ask questions in secret with trusted friends or in dark corners of the internet. It had become apparent that those in spiritual authority over us could no longer be considered *safe*.

Three

Wendell Berry's book *Jayber Crow* tells the fictitious story of a young orphan who grew up to become the barber in a small town after realizing he had too many questions to become a preacher. That growing pile of questions about life and God became unmanageable during his time at seminary, culminating in a fortuitous meeting with the dean of men.

"I've got a lot of questions."

He said, "Perhaps you would like to say what they are?"

"Well, for instance," I said, "if Jesus said for us to love our enemies—and He did say that, didn't He?—how can it ever be right to *kill* our enemies? And if He said not to pray in public, how come we're all the time praying in public? And if Jesus' own prayer in the garden wasn't granted, what is there for us to pray, except 'thy will be done,' which there's no use in praying because it will be done anyhow?"

I sort of ran down. He didn't say anything. He was looking straight at me. And then I realized that he wasn't looking at me the way he usually did. I seemed to see way back in his eyes a little gleam of light. It was a light of kindness and (as I now think) of amusement.

He said, "Have you any more?"

"Well, for instance," I said, for it had just occurred to me, "suppose you prayed for something and you got it, how do you know *how* you got it? How do you know you didn't get it because you were going to get it whether you prayed for it or not? So how do you know it does any good to pray? You would need proof, wouldn't you?"

He nodded.

"But there's no way to get any proof."

He shook his head. We looked at each other.

He said, "Do you have any answers?"

"No," I said. I was concentrating so hard, looking at him, you could have nailed my foot to the floor and I wouldn't have felt it.

"So," I said, "I reckon what it all comes down to is, how can I preach if I don't have any answers?"

"Yes, Mr. Crow," he said. "How can you?" He was not one of your frying-size chickens.

"I don't believe I can," I said, and I felt my skin turn cold, for I had not even thought that until then."[3]

For the most part, two different audiences will read this book—those on Jayber's side of the conversation, and those on the dean's side. Many deconstructors know exactly what it is like to sit across the table from those in spiritual authority and explain themselves to the critics who pound them with questions they cannot answer to their satisfaction. Critics often have more questions than there are actual answers. And then deconstructors wonder how their own questions will be received. Will those who ask questions exercise power over them, forcing them to choose between honest intellectual pursuit and blind ideology?

Another way to say this looks like this: *whistleblowers rarely end up as heroes for telling the truth.* Telling the truth in many Christian institutions is the fastest way to become persona non grata, which almost rhymes with piranha. Those in power often gather patriots in their corner to exercise the power of exclusion, false accusations, and denunciation. In all this, the light of Christ, the truth, and the gospel are covered up.

Continuing the Journey

Both of us have sat across the table from pilgrims who have unpacked their bags for us, showing us the burdens and questions they carry and asking how they can continue the journey when their pack gets heavier and heavier. We can see it in their eyes. They are deciding if they want to retreat or push forward. Whether we like it or not, we are children of the Enlightenment, and we want answers to our questions and the evidence to back them up. And while there have been occasions for us to provide answers (sometimes there *are* good answers), most of the time we nod to those who pour out their questions, remembering when we were forced to deal with the mysteries of faith ourselves.

Sometimes we're able to help people move further into faith by directing them to theologians who have waded into the murky waters of doubt and whose writings have guided spiritual pilgrims for hundreds, even thousands, of years. But there have been times when we have had to help people find their way out of the church, gently, in a way that honors their journey with us while leaving the door open for the journey back. And we do believe the journey will bring them back, because we believe that when someone walks away from the church, Jesus goes with them.

Too many people settle for simplistic answers instead of wrestling with disrupting questions. We have seen Christlike people pushed out of churches and Christian institutions for asking questions that disrupt the status quo (and often the flow of money into church coffers). We have seen funding pulled from ministries because a wealthy donor has decided his money qualifies him to put his thumb on the scales when theology and doctrine are being discussed. We have seen good pastors driven out of ministry because they attacked a church's idol or leaned on a sacred cow, whether social, theological, or cultural. How many have been escorted to the door of the church because their questions don't fit in?

We like what Old Testament professor Michelle Knight wrote on Threads:

> Curiosity is not the enemy of certainty.
> Creativity doesn't challenge orthodoxy.
> Conversations need not lead to compromise.
> Questions don't pose a threat to truth.
> Curiosity marks souls who want more than we can imagine. Creativity rejoices in our capacity to grow. Conversations cultivate empathy (and the right kind of compromise!). Questions require humility.
> These virtues are the very foundation of life before God, virtues that curb our thirst for autonomy and train us to glorify Another.[4]

Though he was never called Reverend or held the office of pastor, Jayber Crow pastored people. He became the town barber and listened, speaking into the lives of those who came in, one head of hair at a time. The work of a barber can be priestly. They place their hands on the head of a person in need of refreshment, and the one sitting in that barber's chair can confess the difficulties of life to someone who will carefully remove what is too heavy for them to carry, the sins that have grown and become visible, messy, or unkempt. That person walks out lighter and fresher, with a fresh shave, a crisp haircut, and a new self-image. It's what it should be like as we walk out of a good church service where we feel inspired to live rather than to hide and sulk. There are many ways to *shepherd* and *be shepherded*, which has some wondering why they need the church at all.

Jayber never again set foot in a church to worship because he didn't have a place there. Instead, he took the church to the people in tangible and beautiful ways. Berry's story speaks to our propensity to believe that God works only in the church, not on the streets. Perhaps this is why we sometimes feel like Jesus is invisible in our churches. Maybe he's hanging out at the barbershop, at work through the barber. The light can be brighter outside the church than inside.

I love how Berry ends Jayber Crow's conversation with the dean of men at the seminary, bringing together elements of both mystery and hope:

I said, "Well," for now I was ashamed, "I had this feeling maybe I had been called."

"And you may have been right. But not to what you thought. Not to what you think. You have been given questions to which you cannot be *given* answers. You will have to live them out—perhaps a little at a time."

"And how long is that going to take?"

"I don't know. As long as you live, perhaps."[5]

Berry pushes us to recognize what many deconstructors are coming to terms with—that God's work is not only done by the minister, the pastor, or the one with an office in a church. God's work is done by *anyone and everyone who follows the way mapped by Jesus*. Followers of Jesus, however, can get into a heap of trouble in a church when the church systemically is not following Jesus.

Sealioning Jesus

Have you ever heard of sealioning? It's not in every dictionary yet. Here's an image to help you understand it. If you've ever been in the San Francisco Bay, you may have seen a herd of sea lions emerge from the water, dip and dive, appearing and reappearing, until you're not sure if you keep seeing the same sea lion or another one. Answer: it's not just one; it's several.

The baffling experience of attempting to identify which sea lion is popping up from the water gave rise to a term for a way of responding to someone, often an online troll, when that person is giving someone else a hard time. To sealion someone is to pester them with questions *without staying long enough to hear the person's answer*. Instead of asking genuine questions that lead to genuine conversation, the sealion pops up with a question here, dips and dives, and then reappears for another question, all in an effort to wear people down with endless questions.

We can conclude the questions aren't genuine because the one being questioned is given no time to answer the questions, and the sealion either has no time or interest in the answer. Instead of engaging the ideas under discussion, the sealion spits out gotcha accusations in the form of questions. Sealioning has no interest in the light of truth. Sealioning is pure accusation.

We see this in the Bible as well, in the eighth chapter of John (8:12–59, to be exact). Here we have a long passage that is nothing less than the powers that be sealioning Jesus.

Jesus opened with a wildly big claim: "I am the light of the world" (John 8:12). He intensified that claim by saying, "Whoever follows me will never walk in darkness, but will have the light of life." Since self-claims don't always stand up, his opponents replied, "Here you are, appearing as your own witness." So Jesus gave a more than reasonable response: "I know where I came from. . . . I stand with the Father, who sent me" (8:14, 16). Here, Jesus is claiming he has two witnesses—himself and God the Father.

We see the leaders then leap to another question (beginning to sealion Jesus). "Where is your father?" Jesus shifted lanes slightly by answering, "You do not know me" and if you did, "you would know my Father also" (John 8:19). That's heavy.

Then Jesus pointed a long, long finger at his critics and said, "You are from below; I am from above. You are from this world; I am not of this world." Their response earns an award for question of the year: "Who are you?" Jesus didn't answer his critics directly, but a few verses later, he spoke of himself as "the Son of Man" (John 8:23, 25, 28).

Finally, to the believing Judeans listening to him, Jesus made this promise: "If you hold to my teaching, you are really my disciples. Then you will know the truth, and the truth will set you free" (John 8:31–32). John wanted us to think Jesus' critics just don't get it, so he recorded their failure to understand freedom. They say, "We . . . have never been slaves of anyone" (8:33). Jesus turns their word *slaves* to being *slaves of sin*, and that slaves are not family members, but the Son is—and the Son can set them free.

We could go on. The point is that *it doesn't matter what Jesus* says, *because they have a response*. And frankly, it doesn't matter what they say either, because Jesus has a response. In all that he says, Jesus informs them that he is from the Father and the Father has sent him. They can't buy his claims, so they label him with the worst of labels—that he is "a Samaritan and demon-possessed" (John 8:48). They mention Abraham, and before long, Jesus has made the ultimate claim: "Before Abraham was born, I am!" (8:58).

John tells us that "at this, they picked up stones to stone him" (8:59). In their view, Jesus was speaking blasphemy. Which is precisely the point. Jesus has made some colossally important self-claims—and they have denied him all the way down. The entire chapter is not pretty. It's a heated back-and-forth that turns ugly. But underneath all the questions there is but one issue: *Who is this Jesus?*

If Jesus is who says he is as recorded in John 8, the church has some answering to do.

Sealioning Deconstructors

Sadly, many deconstructors who ask questions of the modern church have a sealion experience similar to Jesus' interactions with the religious leaders of his day. When you are sealioned, it doesn't matter what you say; it will never be good enough. And if your response is a good pushback, the question just changes to an entirely different question. The questions, you soon realize, are not genuine questions; they are criticisms masked as questions, and none of your answers will change the minds of your critics. Sealioning happens when churches train people not to think for themselves or not to think differently from the status quo. Along with that, they teach people not to criticize their leaders, who are, in their own terms, the Lord's anointed.

Deconstructors often have concerns that are just as important, if not more so, than those of their critics. Often, the questions that batter them spring from the bed of ignorance rather than enlightenment. Sealioners may suddenly shift from "Do you believe in a literal six-day creation?" to "Do you think Jonah is a satire, or is it about a real man swallowed by a real fish?" to "Do you think Isaiah wrote all of Isaiah?" to "Are you a Democrat?" and "Do you believe in ordaining women?" to "Are you a universalist?" But again, these questions are not really questions; they are interrogations by an aggressor, accusations with a predetermined verdict.

Questions like these remind me of the early apostles who were on fire for Jesus. Led by Peter, several of them were hauled before the temple authorities. One of the Pharisees (and remember, many Pharisees were intrigued by Jesus) named Gamaliel said something relevant to our discussion: "Therefore, in the present case I advise you: Leave these men alone! Let them go! For if their purpose or activity is of human origin, it will fail. But if it is from God, you will not be able to stop these men; you will only find yourselves fighting against God" (Acts 5:38–39).

We urge church leaders to treat deconstructors in their midst in much the same way as Gamaliel urged the temple authorities to treat the apostles. Call it the "Gamaliel treatment," and make it genuine. We say the same to well-meaning church worriers who think deconstructors are the problem who need to be shut down. If what they are asking questions about—their new convictions—are "of human origin," they will fail. But if they are from God, we will not be able to thwart them. In fact, shutting them out and silencing them will be "fighting against God," who may be speaking to the church *through* the questions of deconstructors. What if God is using the questions and concerns of deconstructors as a prophetic voice to challenge today's church—a church that may bear witness to an invisible Jesus?

The deconstructors we know and have talked with want to see Jesus. They are seeking light in churches that cover the Light of the World. But when the church responds by silencing them, they leave in search of the Light. Perhaps in walking away from the church, they are walking toward the Light.

The Issue Is the Light

In the Gospel of John, we find several I Am statements, including "I am the light of the world" (John 8:12), and concluding with one of the most powerful of all. Jesus declared, "Before Abraham was born, I am" (8:58). Here Jesus claims both to be *in* the light and to *be* the Light. The intensity and depth of Jesus' claims are what matter here. Deconstructing are asking, "What place will Jesus have in the church?" We think this is *the* question of our generation.

Jesus claims to be the Light, but is Jesus the light in our churches? And if he is not, who is the light? What is the light? These are questions that can often be answered with "the pastor" or "the pastor's theology," or even "this favorite author" or "that author's belief system." The only way through the darkness is with the Light of all lights. We are not united by our grasp of light, but by being gripped by the Light himself. What might happen when our churches, programs, and day-to-day life together draw their energy and their beliefs from the Light, *who is a person and not just a set of ideas*?

The answer, we're convinced, is that everything changes.

Light, in the statement "I am the light of the world," is a metaphor for truth, for wisdom, knowing God, and knowing how best to live in this world. Jesus claims to be the Light of the world, which means he is for the whole world. In an effort to get everyone's attention, Jesus assigns the world to "darkness." John 8 is an intense section in which Jesus uses either-ors without nuance. It's an above and below, light and darkness, truth and lie, this world against the Father's side. One is either enslaved or free, a child of Jesus' Father or of the devil.

While we must be cautious in how we apply these harsh binaries (these polar opposites can become dangerous language in the hands of bad people, as we saw in the Holocaust against the Jews) we dare not minimize this language. As many have observed, this was how ancient people expressed their deepest disagreements. We can understand what Jesus is saying without replicating that harshness in our own rhetoric.

Still, the issue drills down to one question yet again: *Who is this man?* If he is the Light, who is he? The entire passage is about Jesus. Deconstructors are deeply serious about Jesus, but equally certain he has left the house (the church). For many of them, there's not enough of Jesus in the church so they've gone in search of him elsewhere. How might understanding the reality that Jesus is the Light of the world shed light on what a Jesus-based church can be?

The Light Is Bright

Jesus is the Light in that he *knows* God. He also knows us, shining his light on human beings and human nature. He reveals who God is by embodying God. He unmasks the powers and reveals the power of love.

Jesus shined soul-piercing light into hidden places:

on hypocrisy
on greed
on powermongering
on loopholes in legislation
on hatred of one's enemies
on dodgy words
on people claiming to be God's special people but don't act
    like it
on narcissists clamoring for glory and power
on Rome's imperial violence
on ignoring the hurting and wounded

Jesus also shined kingdom-nurturing light:

on the true way of life
on the poor who trust in God
on the meek and humble
on the merciful
on the heart-pure folks
on peacemakers
on widows who gave their all
on the demonized searching for liberation
on women looking to advance the kingdom of God
on the socially ostracized looking for social welcome
on a Gentile woman who wanted her daughter back alive

These very concerns drive many deconstructors to ask the
questions they ask and seek Jesus like they do. They want God's

light to shine brightly, even if means exposure. They want it to shine brightly, especially to reveal the hidden followers of Jesus who are otherwise unknown, invisible, and ignored. They want light to flood the room and chase away darkness. They want to experience with one another the light of love. They want a bright community filled with Jesus' light.

Deconstructors, in other words, are witnesses to the vision of Jesus that he is the Light of the World. The God they believe in is seen in Jesus, the Light, and they want the Light to shine in the darkness. Since they have experienced the covering of the Light, they are on the move, looking for a place filled with light.

Seeing Jesus at the Door

Doors are simple. To be sure, some are beautiful, like the doors on cathedrals in Italy that are designed to be decorative— some of the most beautiful ones you'll ever see. If you drive through the neighborhoods of the rich and famous, you might spy doors on mansions designed to impress others and protect those in power and their wealth. But every door has one of two primary simple purposes—to keep someone in and/or to keep someone out. Often, the door does both at the same time.

When we tell someone, "I'll show you the door," we're typically not bragging about the design of the door. We're using it metaphorically to mean "show someone the exit." Doors often have a metaphorical connotation of entering or exiting. Search for *door* on Amazon, and you'll learn about *The Millionaire Next Door*, *The Door of No Return*, *A Wind in the Door*, *The Doors of Perception*, and *Europe through the Back Door*. Many years ago, some of us may have read James Sire's *The Universe Next Door*. None of these are referring to a literal, physical door. Each of them utilizes the word *door* as a metaphor for entering or exiting.

Out the Door

We know families and individuals who have been shown the door, asked in no uncertain terms to leave the church. They've been sidelined and sabotaged. The message was clear: you are not welcome here. Some were shown the door when they shared that their daughter or son is LGBTQ+. Some deconstructors have walked out the door of their church after being hurt by harsh messages about sexuality while messages of justice for the poor and challenge to the economically privileged are ignored, ignored, and ignored.

Professors have been shown the door (or walked out before being shown the door) because their beliefs didn't dot the right *i* or land on the correct conviction. We know followers of Jesus who walked out the door because they were scandalized by the overt hypocrisy of church leaders or couldn't abide the complaint culture of those in the inner circle. Some pastors have watched hundreds walk out the doors of their churches because they have chosen to embrace one political party over another. And there's one church we know whose weekly attendance dropped in half when it transitioned from the "get as many as we can to church each Sunday" mindset to a model where all its energies are directed toward the transformation of people into Christlikeness.

Entire groups in our culture have been shown the door in that they have become invisible to those who remain on the inside. White churches have shown the door (by failing to welcome and include) to African and Mexican and Asian Americans. Ralph

Ellison wrote one of the most searing, haunting novels called *Invisible Man*. Here's how the unnamed—so invisible is he—man describes himself as he opens the door to the invisible:

> I am an invisible man. No, I am not a spook like those who haunted Edgar Allan Poe; nor am I one of your Hollywood-movie ectoplasms. I am a man of substance, of flesh and bone, fiber and liquids—and I might even be said to possess a mind. I am invisible, understand, simply because people refuse to see me. Like the bodiless heads you see sometimes in circus sideshows, it is as though I have been surrounded by mirrors of hard, distorting glass. When they approach me they see only my surroundings, themselves, or figments of their imagination—indeed, everything and anything except me.
>
> Nor is my invisibility exactly a matter of a biochemical accident to my epidermis. That invisibility to which I refer occurs because of a peculiar disposition of the eyes of those with whom I come in contact. A matter of the construction of their *inner* eyes, those eyes with which they look through their physical eyes upon reality. I am not complaining, nor am I protesting either. It is sometimes advantageous to be unseen, although it is most often rather wearing on the nerves. . . . Or again, you doubt if you really exist. You wonder if you aren't simply a phantom in other people's minds.[1]

If you aren't already familiar with this story, it's about a Black man in twentieth-century America. And it's the same story today, only worse. A Black person's skin color is their uniform, the one they can never take off. When an African American pastor friend first used the "uniform" image in my hearing, it stunned me.

Think about it. White people don't have a uniform that stands out from others because most of the time they are in environments where everyone else—or at least a large majority—is wearing the same uniform. When a White woman enters the door of the church, she's seen as a possible member. But when a Black woman enters the door, she's seen as Black. And when a young Black man with a cocked hat enters the door, the leaders go on high alert. The message communicated all too often is, *Why did he enter our door?*

Far more often than many White church leaders realize, deconstructors walk out the door of their church because of systemic racism—either visibly present in the church or in the lack of a voice that resists it. I know that for some of you, those are fighting words, so I'll say something to the flag raisers. It's true. America is systemically White in its economy, its politics, its power, its jobs, and the majority of its churches. The ironic cry that many raise today is that progressives and deconstructors are "woke." But this is itself a racist remark that proves what they claim—the existence of systemic racism.

To apply that label to others enables ongoing racism in that culture and keeps the system in place. It allows individuals to stay blind to injustice and prejudice. The systemic powers in the institutional White church continue to be sustained by the lack of awareness—or even a willingness to consider the existence—of White power.

Many of those who have walked out the back door of the church have chosen to enter the front door of another church—a more inclusive church. It may be a house church, a Thursday evening group that meets at a local bar or at someone's home, or an urban church where diversity mirrors the neighborhoods around it. A church where Jesus opens the door for them. Let this be said:

> The country is rapidly becoming a multiethnic, pluralistic, egalitarian nation, where women and men are increasingly seen as equal. . . . By 2060, according to projections from the Census Bureau, only 43 percent of Americans will be white. Twenty-eight percent will be Hispanic, 15 percent will be Black, 9 percent will be Asian American, and 6 percent will come from two or more ethnic backgrounds.[2]

Jesus opens the door for all because he knows each of them by name. Deconstructors who have been shown the door are looking for that Door of welcome. They know Jesus is more welcoming than the church they have left.

The Door Is a Person

Twice in John 10, Jesus said, "I am the gate" (10:7, 9). In the same chapter, he is also the "good shepherd" (10:11). (The Greek term translated "gate" in some modern English translations is used most often for a "door," so we're going to follow that translation as we move forward. Besides, we think of gates as rickety old things.) Doors are not the point here—it's what they do, how they function. Doors open spaces and close spaces. They keep things in or permit things to enter. Here we learn that Jesus *is* the Door, so the door is both the point (it's all about Jesus) and not the point (Jesus leads to new spaces). Jesus is not only the door to the pen for the sheep, but he is also the Good Shepherd (10:11), which means readers need to see Jesus doing double duty here.

English teachers will tell us a good shepherd and a door are images that don't mesh well—they collide with one another. Mixed metaphors. We can answer back, "Yes, English teacher, you are right, but we get the gist. Let's move on." Jesus both opens and closes the door, and he cares for the sheep. We can think of him as the Good Shepherd-Door (or something like that).

But what does it mean to say Jesus is both the Door and the Good Shepherd? In combining the uncombinable, Jesus creates an opportunity for others to enter into the family of God. They enter through him in order to be with him and experience the abundant life.

But what's on the far side of the door when the door is Jesus?

Petty Pastors and Their Doordom

When deconstructors say the church needs to be more about Jesus, they speak prophetically, reminding us that Jesus is both the Door and the Good Shepherd. The only story the church is empowered to tell is the story about Jesus. Not a story primarily about the church, the musicians, the preacher, or another plat-formed personality. Branding the church or those on the platform pushes Jesus off the platform. We are not the message. We are not the mission. And we are certainly not the main attraction. Jesus is. Deconstructors have opted out of church because the church is missing the main attraction. When the pastor or the church becomes the main attraction, Jesus becomes invisible.

At the time of Jesus—and continuing in our day—thieves and bandits most often entered the sheepfold by climbing over the fence. They were not welcome at the gate because they did not know the gatekeeper, and the gatekeeper recognized them as invaders and intruders (John 10:3). Becoming a spiritual door for another, which is what spiritual leaders are called to be and do, requires trust. Trust forms over time.

Jesus, the Good Shepherd, is the only door for entering the sheepfold of the church. Toxic teachers and church leaders open the door to their own "doordom," assuming authority and violating the consciences of trusting, vulnerable persons. Toxic leaders capture people through manipulation, engendering loyalty while stealing minds and money. Their ego directs their aims; loyalty is their rallying cry; tribalism forms their mission.

They drive people who disagree out the door instead of to the Door—Jesus. They are today's thieves and bandits (John 10:1), and Jesus denounces them as hired hands (10:12–13), suggesting they are only in it for the money. Jesus says these toxic leaders don't care at all about the sheep (10:13). Many deconstructors can sense these leaders with their fragile egos, recognizing them for what they are—usurpers of Jesus the Door.

Over the past several decades, one leader after another has collapsed before the watching world. And as they fall into the waters of toxicity, they splash their dirty water all over the Nones, Dones, and deconstructors. Many of these same deconstructors are the very ones pointing out these toxicities and corruptions.

Yet instead of humbling themselves in the face of truth and confessing the error of their ways, toxic leaders work their board into a defense, mimicking a plea for loyalty and the good of the gospel's reputation, turning against the whistleblowers and blaming them. They surround themselves with their defenders and thereby convince themselves they are in the right. They do all they can to change the narrative from a story about their sin to a story about their critics.

If you've never heard the phrase DARVO, do a search. Then, remember it when you watch the next leader fall. DARVO is an acronym that stands for "**d**eny, **a**ccuse, then **r**everse the **v**ictim and **o**ffender." And DARVO happens when those accused have the power to narrate the "official" story, and they turn the offender into the victim and the true victim into the offender. Deconstructors have had enough of these false narratives and flipping of the script. Why trust the pastor who preaches forgiveness of sins for those who confess but *who can't confess their own sins*? Who turns their sin into the sin of the one calling it out? Who turns the whistleblower into the perpetrator?

In the summer of 2019, I (Tommy) sent a group text to my friends that included a link to a new Instagram account called PreachersNSneakers. At the time, it had around five thousand followers, with more joining every hour. The content struck a nerve with many young deconstructors. Seeing the images on the account, they immediately recognized a snapshot of what Christianity-at-large had become. It was filled with pictures of pastors, usually mid-sermon, zooming in on a closeup of their shoes, belts, jackets, jeans, and watches. Along with the pictures was a list of the clothing items and, most importantly, what they cost. As of this writing, the account has more than 346,000 followers.

With each post, followers were shocked. The pastors and church leaders profiled grew uneasy and upset. Many followers noted the ironic contrast between what the pastors wore and the message they proclaimed—a message about a homeless, itinerant preacher who said he had come "to proclaim good news to the poor" (Luke 4:18). The pastors were angry because the account exposed their behavior, rendering their beliefs and words impotent. Several pastors sent threatening "cease and desist" messages, while others battled it out in the comment section (typically making things far worse for themselves). The contrast between the message and the messenger was obvious.

Jesus is the Door, and if our lives aren't inviting people to enter through the Jesus Door rather than the Look-at-me Door, something is wrong.

The Church's Fake Doors

When I (Tommy) started out as a pastor, a retired clergyman pulled me aside and said, "What you save someone with is what you are saving them to." It may have been a well-known axiom, but I had never heard it before. So it didn't mean much to me—until I saw it happen.

If churches draw people in via the door of *social media*, they will learn that its methods of attraction create social media Christianity—a form of Christianity filled with titillations, controversies, accusations, and a lack of interest in truth and listening to others. My (Scot's) pastor has said several times that social media is spiritual formation, whether it forms us for good or for bad. And she's right. It's scary to consider how spending days and nights on Twitter barking at others forms us spiritually, but it does. Sometimes under a pseudonym. Oy!

Other churches have a door that appeals to *culture* and *patriotism* to draw you in. They may draw boundaries around particular political stances or cultural traditions, marking those things "Christian" and other things "secular" or "socialist." They may blame foreigners for cultural problems. When people are drawn in through the door of culture and patriotism, they may struggle to believe that God is at work in and through other cultures. A recent study showed that many dechurched Southern cultural Christians have now become Southern political populists.[3] Churches with their door shaped by patriotism often can't distinguish between populist politics and the gospel.

Many of those who are now deconstructors grew up as evangelical youth group kids in the 1980s and '90s. They were drawn in by marketing, raffles, entertaining Wednesday nights, and late-night Friday rock shows in the church basement. They were sold a *consumerist* view of the church that connected godliness with wealth, celebrity, and success. The churches they were raised in formed them to believe that if they avoided sin—especially sexual sins—and were outspoken about their beliefs, then God would grant the rewards that had drawn them to the church— material blessings, numerical growth, and success. And, of course, a smokin' hot wife or husband.

The very things their leaders exploited to draw kids through the church's door became the rewards that drove them forward in faith. Perhaps if their spiritual leaders drew them in with Christlikeness, they would have been drawn *to* Christlikeness. But they were given no cross to carry; no call to love our enemies; no challenges to greed, luxury, and the American Dream; and no Spirit to follow through the wilderness of temptation.

The tragedy inevitably came when success didn't. When friends remained "sexually pure" but carried so much baggage from purity culture that their marriages failed. When the promised joy that children would bring ended with a child's illness or death. When the money ran out, poverty crept in and faith began to slip away. Deconstruction occurs when the faith we were sold no longer works as promised, when we no longer have anything to hold on to. Many were drawn in with sneakers, status, and promises of blessings. But there was no Jesus. And deconstruction finds us when Jesus goes invisible.

What leads us toward Christlikeness is a church door called Jesus. If you save people with Jesus by teaching what he taught and living as his followers, they will not turn to other doors, such as patriotism, anarchism, conservatism, liberalism, capitalism, Marxism, or socialism. They will turn to Jesus. This is the only way we know to build deconstruction-proof churches. And ironically, many of today's deconstructors are camped out at Jesus' door after their church showed them *the* door.

Jesus is more than the Door. He is the Good Shepherd-Door. He is the true pastor. And many today long for a Jesus-like pastor.

What to Look for When Looking for a Pastor

If you are on a search committee or are simply looking for a new church to escape a toxic leader and team, remember that the typical first impressions don't count. Most pastors can platform well. If they couldn't, they wouldn't be on the platform. So you're wise to ignore or look past the attributes of performance. Wait, listen, watch, and discern. Yes, it takes time. Don't rush to judgment or be in a hurry. Hold back. Pray about it. Think about it. Ask good questions.

Begin with a good definition of a pastor—one who lives out the life of Jesus in your midst in a way you can follow. In other words, a pastor should be someone who nurtures you into becoming more like Jesus. Please avoid the temptation to think of a pastor as a CEO, an organization guru, or a motivational speaker. They should be the presence of Christ for the community. They gather, teach, and offer the body and blood for salvation and the forgiveness of sins. And their life makes the cross and the broken body of Christ visible and tangible in ways that bring about restoration and resurrection.

The foremost attribute to look for in a pastor is Spirit-shaped Christlikeness, someone who has followed the Spirit of God in such a way that the fruit of the Spirit is visible on the tree that is their life. A good pastor is *loving* and *joyful*, not constantly angry or defensive. They are *peaceful* (both on and off social media) and *patient* with people. A good pastor avoids anxiety about the long, slow journey of faith. A good pastor's spirit and presence are *kind* and *good*. Such virtues will also permeate the culture of the church, building an ethos in which people not only do good and kind things, but *are* good and kind people. As you spend time in that church community, ask yourself if the people are good, kind, peaceful, patient, joyful, and loving.

Look for a *faithful* person. Pastoring is more than a job; it is a calling in and for the community. A pastor is involved in marrying, burying, baptizing, baby dedicating, and guiding people through the highs and lows of life together. This requires presence. A good pastor relates to people with *gentleness*. People carry brokenness and must be handled gently, so the cracks won't spread and the brokenness won't grow. A gentle pastor walks into people's lives quietly and only when invited. They open doors slowly and carry extra grace in their pocket. They are not harsh, judgmental, or someone to be feared; gentleness neither condemns nor threatens.

Lastly, look for *self-control*. In the Greek world, self-control meant making decisions from a both passion and reason held in balance so that you were led neither by cold reasoning nor hot passions. Self-control makes decisions that take into account both the wisdom of the church (the past) and the coming kingdom of God (the future). They do not make decisions impulsively or on a whim. Good pastors are driven not by dopamine but by the wisdom of the ages.

Finally, ask yourself two questions. First, *do I want to become like this pastor?* Pastors leave footprints in the sand for others to follow. If your sons and daughters follow those footsteps and become like this pastor, will you be pleased? I often meet people who express fear of their pastor, and then I watch as, over time, their children come to fear their parents. You become like your pastor.

Second, *do I want to read the Bible as this pastor reads it?* You learn how to read the Bible like the people you read the Bible *with*. If a pastor interprets the Bible harshly or if the reading is unloving, such is yours likely to become. A reading that bores you will turn people toward the back door. A reading of the Bible that subjugates women will subjugate others. A reading of the Bible that condemns others will eventually condemn you because it is a reading that allows condemnation. If you don't want to read the Bible in a way that subjugates and condemns, then don't follow a pastor who promotes such readings in the church. Look for a pastor who reads the Bible widely, generously, accurately, lovingly, peacefully, gently, joyfully, and kindly. To summarize, a good pastor is one who lives like Jesus and wants others to join in the journey of learning together how to live like Jesus.

In *Death in Holy Orders*, novelist P. D. James sketches the realities of actual pastoral care, the kind of shepherd care exercised by Jesus. Those who love people like this pastor find a door that leads to Jesus. About the pastor, James writes:

He had returned from two hours of visiting long-term sick
and housebound parishioners. As always he had tried con-
scientiously to meet their individual and predictable needs:
blind Mrs. Oliver, who liked him to read a passage of scripture
and pray with her; old Sam Possinger, who on every visit re-
fought the Battle of Alamein; Mrs. Poley, caged in her Zimmer
frame, avid for the latest parish gossip; Carl Lomas, who had
never set foot in St. Botolph's but liked discussing theology
and the defects of the Church of England. Mrs. Poley, with
his help, had edged her way painfully into the kitchen and
made tea, taking from the tin the gingerbread cake she had
baked for him. He had unwisely praised it four years ago, on
his first visit, and was now condemned to eat it weekly, finding
it impossible to admit that he disliked gingerbread. But the
tea, hot and strong, had been welcome and would save him the
trouble of making it at home.[4]

When the shepherd metaphor is put into practice, it looks a
lot like what James describes here. The Nones, Dones, and deconstructors all want and need a spiritual sage who cares enough for
them to be their pastor, to listen to their sighs, hurts, relational
struggles, and intellectual questions. They're looking, but are
they finding these caring pastors in churches, or do they need to
go elsewhere? We close this chapter with a story of a pastor who
listened carefully to a deconstructor.

Pastors Listen

One of the more unnervingly difficult things about deconstruction is the occasional and, at times, relentless desire to go back

to the way things were, back to the time when faith was vibrant and filled with joy, back to feeling like we understood God, the Bible, the church, and the ins-and-outs of theology and doctrine. I (Tommy) once sat with a young man in his early thirties as he recounted and lamented his losses during his deconstruction journey. He lost his place of prominence in the community because he wouldn't side with them on a particular issue they deemed paramount. He lost his friends—those he came to find out were talking behind his back about how he had "gone liberal." He missed having peaceful holiday visits with his parents, who became invasive with their questions, sealioning him for hours about his faith, to the point where he could no longer have the kind of deep and meaningful conversations he was used to having with them.

Through tears, he explained he had been an apologist, a reasoner, and an intellectual. But now he found himself unable to defend Christianity, God, the Bible, or the church: "The first thing to go was my desire and ability to do apologetics. None of it needed defending. In fact, it needs much more scrutiny so that I can somehow figure out if it is true or not. So I stopped defending it, and I walked over to the other side and started attacking it myself."

This is not a rare occurrence, and if you've ever found yourself having a debate with exvangelicals online, you may well have been debating someone who has experienced this very pain.

And it's not just relationships that suffer. The center of being is lost with faith. I (Tommy) remember a loved one saying something similar while we sat on my front porch late one night:

I don't even bother to pray anymore. It no longer makes sense to me. I used to pray all day long. Prayer was the thing that filled me up. But now I don't know what the point is, and I don't know what to tell the kids when they ask me to pray with them at night. I simply go through the motions. I miss the connection I once had through prayer, but that connection was severed when I threw out my old faith structure. I tried to pray, but it feels like there's no one there.

Jesus is the Door. Jesus is the Good Shepherd. The Good Shepherd-Door knows each of us by name. The Door he welcomes us. The Good Shepherd knows and cares for us in our needs. What deconstructors want are mentor pastors who know them and care for them, who listen to them. Some in the pew may wrongly believe deconstruction is cool or sexy. But when you talk with those in any phase of deconstruction, you will likely hear pain, angst, and disorienting liminality. At times they don't know where to find themselves on the spiritual map.

This is why we urge you, especially if you are a pastor or church leader, to listen to them. We believe the future of the church is connected to their questions and the answers they discover. This, too, is part of deconstruction—us learning to care for them, just as Jesus does.

Encountering Jesus
in the Shepherd

Sean McDowell is the son of an uber-famous Christian apologist, Josh McDowell, the whippersnapper (at the time) who wrote the bestselling book, *Evidence That Demands a Verdict*. When I (Scot) was in college, everyone I knew was reading McDowell. Yes, everyone. And I did too. When Josh's son Sean was in college, however, Sean began to doubt his faith, and it got very difficult for him to believe some of the things he once believed. He was unnerved about it, and his doubts were deep enough he wanted to talk to Mr. Famous Apologist Dad himself. Here are Sean's own words:

As we sat in a small café in the mountains of Breckenridge, Colorado, I told my dad about my doubts. His response took me by surprise. "I think it's great that you want to find the truth," he said. "It's wise not to accept things just because you were told them. You need to find out for yourself if you think

Christianity is true. You know that your mom and I love you regardless of what you conclude. Seek after the truth, and take to heart the things your mom and I have taught you. And let me know if I can help along the way."[1]

This is a good response to a doubting son or daughter. We wonder how many others would have had an easier time with their deconstruction and questioning if they had parents who responded as Sean's father responded. (All of them.)

Deconstruction is nothing new. It has always been part of the life of Christian believers in the church and part of church history. Those trying to shut down the questioning voices are ignorant of the patterns of upheaval and reformation that have emerged throughout Christian history. At times these upheavals have also followed the discovery of widespread patterns of toxic pastors and priests. Hear this story of a young man in the United States:

I was ten years old. My brother, who is eight years my junior, was very ill in an intensive care unit. The pastor came in and looked at my folks, and I was standing right there, and he said, "Someone in this family has committed some awful sin for God to visit this sort of judgment." I can remember it and take you to that spot today. I haven't said that in years, and it takes my breath away just to say it.[2]

Statements like this flow from teachers who are ill-formed in both their theology and their character. We can't say this any more compassionately or truthfully: this kind of "theology" damages and ruins faith. Churches fall apart with heartlessness like this.

People leave churches over statements like this. Deconstructors feel the weight of pastoral actions like this (if you can even call it pastoral—we don't).

In her book *The Great Emergence*, Phyllis Tickle wrote about the life cycle of the church throughout history, emphasizing how there seems to be a pattern to the great upheavals the church experiences, much like the one we are experiencing today. She points back five hundred years to the Protestant Reformation and says, "If then, five hundred years back from our time takes us to the Great Reformation, where does five hundred years back from the Great Reformation take us? Obviously to the Great Schism."[3] The pattern keeps going back further: "Five hundred years prior to the Great Schism takes us to the sixth century and what once upon a very recent time was labeled as 'The Fall of the Roman Empire,' or 'The Coming of the Dark Ages.'"[4] And, of course, five hundred years before that was the ministry of Jesus of Nazareth—the greatest religious upheaval of all.

Creating five-hundred-year cycles may be a little too convenient and, at times, a stretch of a nuanced reality, but one cannot deny her larger point—some major upheavals have happened. Upheavals always involve some form of *de*construction and *re*construction.

Tickle refers to these times of upheaval and reformation as rummage sales (we call them yard sales), where the things that have become useless to the church are dragged out onto the metaphorical church lawn and offered up behind a sign that reads, "Everything must go!" During these times, many strongly held ideas are lifted up to the Light of the World, who is Jesus. What survives is what survives, and not much else.

> **Ⓜ Miley — Jul 20**
>
> Deconstruction is like cleaning a closet. You ambitiously start by taking everything out. Then there's so much stuff, you realize this is a way bigger undertaking than you thought. You want to stop, but you're in way too deep. You begin to sort and part with things that may have some sentimental value. It's not easy, but you know it doesn't make sense to keep holding on. You remove the junk, and you find out you can have clarity. You can see the closet in its entirety for the first time. It's making sense. You question why you didn't do it sooner.

Today, many people have noticed there are some not quite full-on rummage sales, but more of a shuffling of the furniture occurring more often than every five hundred years—perhaps every twenty-five years or so. Many people who are middle-aged or older have lived through several little reformations that have felt like recalibrations of church culture.

Toxicity in the Church Leaders

These cycles of rummage sales or deconstruction, or whatever you want to call them, are necessary. They should be seen as part of communal life together as the church. Something yet again is stirring in the church today, with the questions and challenges raised by deconstruction. Inconsistencies are being amplified; abuse is being exposed; and paper-thin doctrinal positions are being ripped up and decried as hurtful. Perhaps the church is due for another rummage sale. And it may be bigger than some of the previous ones.

With their objections and questions, deconstructors press the church to revise what it looks for in its leaders and pastors. In the church rummage sale of the twenty-first century, one of the big-ticket items getting tossed is the job description defining what a church leader is. Deconstructors ask tough questions about toxic leaders who attempt to impose old-fashioned boundary markers on a new generation.

Over the past several years, my daughter (Laura Barringer) and I (Scot) have listened to, read, and interacted with—and this is a sad truth—hundreds of stories of good people who have been power-abused by pastors, leaders, and toxic systems in churches. This oft-overused sentence still applies: toxic leadership has risen to pandemic levels in many churches. And the bottom line for this toxic leadership pandemic boils down to seven marks:

1. Lack of self-awareness by church leaders, who, truth be told, need to go through a battery of psychological tests to become more self-aware.
2. Egotistical and narcissistic personalities running too many churches.
3. The abuse of power and the grasping for authority in a church by its leaders.
4. Preachers "speaking for God" instead of speaking as one of Jesus' followers.
5. Boards measuring success by butts in the seats, bills in the plate, baptisms in the water, and the size and number of new buildings. (I, Scot, got some of that sentence from a pastor friend.)
6. Pastors gravitating toward role models who are megachurch pastors with megachurch personalities.
7. Preaching replaced by platform performances.

None of this looks like Jesus, sounds like Jesus, or smells like Jesus. Much of this toxicity emerges from the business world and the Western capitalist definition of success. Our pastoral job descriptions are written up to find such persons.

We need a rummage sale to unload toxic leaders and cultures. The problem of toxic leadership has become so important among deconstructors that we now have a new label for it: spiritual abuse.

> Spiritual abuse is a form of emotional and psychological abuse. It is characterized by a systematic pattern of coercive and controlling behaviour in a religious context. Spiritual abuse can have a deeply damaging impact on those who experience it.
>
> This abuse may include: manipulation and exploitation, enforced accountability, censorship of decision making, requirements for secrecy and silence, coercion to conform, [inability to ask questions], control through the use of sacred texts or teaching, requirement of obedience to the abuser, the suggestion that the abuser has a "divine" position, isolation as a means of punishment, and superiority and elitism.[5]

We perceive spiritual abuse as we recognize the asymmetry of power that a pastor or spiritual leader has and how that power can be wielded in a way that abuses and wounds a person who has less power. Spiritual abuse includes the *neglect of pastoral care* by a pastor. One of my intuitions about deconstructors is that they have not only recognized but personally experienced the widespread absence of pastoral care, attention, and mentoring from pastors. Few pastors consider personal pastoral care a high priority, except in situations of crisis. The prophet Ezekiel railed against such spiritual leaders in his day: "You have not strengthened the weak or healed the sick or bound up the injured. You have not brought back the strays or searched for the lost. You have ruled them harshly and brutally" (Ezekiel 34:4).

While this is a very old text, one cannot find a more piercing criticism of spiritual neglect as a form of spiritual abuse.[6] One item in Ezekiel's catalogue of spiritual abuse immediately grabs our attention: the abusive leader's behavior prompts the sheep— the people—to walk out the door, run away, and scatter.

In the above definition of spiritual abuse, notice the "divine position" a pastor has. Add to this the widespread perception that a pastor has a special connection with God. It is not a terribly big jump from "my pastor" to "voice of God" to "authority from God." Our perceptions of God's relationship with us funnel through the pastoral leaders we experience. This is great if you have a perfect pastor. But there is no such thing as a perfect pastor, and that's why we need to talk about spiritual abuse.

That said, it is easy to toss a phrase like "spiritual abuse" at anyone we don't like. We counsel people to break down spiritual abuse to its three basic elements:

1. The *asymmetry in power* between a person with some kind of spiritual authority and another person.
2. An *observable pattern of abuse*, though a single case can constitute spiritual abuse, and spiritual abuse can at times penetrate a culture so thoroughly it becomes *systemic*.
3. *Behaviors* by a spiritual authority that *psychologically, emotionally, and spiritually wound* a person.

It takes wise leaders to recognize spiritual abuse and handle it well. Spiritual abuse happens. Often. Deconstructors have often experienced spiritual abuse or they know others who have. They are speaking up, urging the church to end spiritual abuse in churches. Some are insisting that churches require background checks for church leaders at all levels. They are demanding that churches and Christian institutions develop and publish whistle-blower policies, host educational programs to inform churches about spiritual abuse, and create policies for independent investigations of allegations. They are asking churches to form policies that protect victims of spiritual abuse. It's embarrassing when pastors resist these healthy developments in their churches. Many who resist the incursion of these suggestions are the ones who have the most to lose.

Jesus Knows Leadership

Not everyone knows what good leadership looks like. Those who grew up with abusive pastors, teachers, or parents often don't have a reference point for knowing what a good leader looks like. They may have no instinct to recognize a good pastor, teacher, or parent, and, as a result, they may grow up looking like the (bad) examples of authority they've witnessed. But the opposite is true as well.

I (Tommy) came across a post on the popular online forum Reddit titled, "What is it like to have loving parents?" By the time I found it, 49,000 people had interacted with that single sentence. The replies ranged from beautiful to heartrending stories about parents. One teenage boy recounted the time his four-year-old sister accidentally broke a Christmas ornament while they were decorating the tree. His mother responded by shouting, "Now I'll destroy something *you* love!" And she did, throwing an object at his sister's tea set, smashing it. The comments contained stories of parental rage, abandonment, and constant threats that a child had better succeed—*or else!*

But I also read beautiful stories from those who experienced healthy families and lovely parents. "I always just felt 100 percent safe," said one commenter. "No matter what happened, I knew everything would be okay." Another commenter stated that when you come from a loving home, you don't have to seek companionship outside of your family because you already have all the love you need. You never feel alone, ever.

The healthy expression of authority from a parent, a teacher, a pastor, and, yes, even a politician can do that. The power they wield can make us feel strong, alive, and able to flourish. It all depends on the character of the one with the power. Remember, spiritual abuse points at an asymmetry of power when the one with spiritual power abuses the one with less power.

There is nothing new about the reality of spiritual abuse, even if the expression itself is new to the dictionary and church discussions. Power has always been intoxicating, and people who like to get intoxicated with power find their way into positions of power. So Jesus' claim to be the *good* shepherd strikingly challenged abuse in his world while also inspiring his own followers not to follow the abuses they had witnessed.

Remember when two of his disciples wanted to be top dogs when the kingdom came (Matthew 20:20–28)? Jesus' words to them were firm, saying essentially, "That's the way of Rome. We are not Rome. Not so among us. We are the way of the cross." He wanted them (and us) to take their leadership class, not from Rome, not from Antipas, not from Pilate, not from Caiaphas, but from Jesus. His way is the way of serving others.

Jesus also gave his disciples two images of toxic leaders—the kind who *rise to power* and the kind who *do wrong by the people*. In John's Gospel, Jesus says that leaders arise in all kinds of ways and with all kinds of motives, both good and bad:

> "Very truly I tell you Pharisees, anyone who does not enter the sheep pen by the gate, but climbs in by some other way, is *a thief and a robber*. The one who enters by the gate is the shepherd of the sheep. The gatekeeper opens the gate for him, and the sheep listen to his voice. He calls his own sheep by name and leads them out." (John 10:1–3, italics added)

Deconstructors have seen too many thieves and robbers in church leadership. They are looking for Jesus-shaped leaders, and if they don't find Jesus-shaped leaders in their church, they exit the door and look for a church with this kind of leader. There are a few stereotypes of bad leaders in Jesus' speech in John's tenth chapter. While he is the Good Shepherd, he is contrasted to what we will refer to as "the grasper" and "the hireling."

The Grasper

One kind of leader who "climbs in by another way" is who we'll call the *grasper*. It's the man or woman who is *grasping at power* and will use any means necessary to attain it, whether by crafting a false identity, using strong-arm tactics, deception, or any number of creative methods to build a following for themselves. They may fake exorcisms or pressure people into exorcisms. They may stage "miracles" or falsify credentials and grade point averages in seminary. Or they may brag about how many books they've read on a subject, thereby making them the authority on it. They love platforms, and you will find them "humbly" trumpeting their newest platform on social media. *I'm so humbled to be invited to speak alongside Celebrity A, Celebrity B, and Celebrity C, when I'm just an ordinary pastor at an ordinary church. It's all because of God.* Those who are aware of these fake public claims of humility know their leaders are just grasping for more platform.

Stealing, killing, violence, and coercion were a regular part of first-century politics. More than 70 percent of Roman emperors died horrific and violent deaths.[7] Why bring up emperors? Because leadership in first-century Judaism was not simply a local leader in a local synagogue with a local congregation. The synagogue was a public assembly hall, as concerned with local politics and social issues as it was with reading and explaining the Torah. The synagogue leaders and teachers had connections to Jerusalem, which had connections to Rome, which meant the Roman emperor's culture impacted and shaped the power culture of Jerusalem and Galilee.

To top it off, the word *shepherd* that Jesus attaches to the word *good*, was as much a metaphor for a king as it was for a local synagogue leader. Not many would notice this, to be sure. But for Jesus to call himself a good shepherd evoked Old Testament passages like Ezekiel 34. The words *king*, *Messiah*, and *shepherd* are all simmering in the pot when Jesus says he is the good shepherd.

The grasper wants to build an audience of loyal followers and then keep them in line. One of their slogans is "building their brand." The grasper spends time every day crafting their public image, chiming in on the latest hot topics of discussion. They post pictures and videos of their messages and put out tweetable one-liners so people will remember and share their thoughts (and social media handle). The grasper becomes arrogant, dismissive of other pastors and leaders, viewing them as rivals rather than partners in ministry. He trades critiques and opinions about all of the other local churches in the city and presents his own church as different, enlightened, advanced. His game is competition, his goal is winning, his aim is glory. Power runs right through all of these. He defends the need for pastoral authority so that he is in charge and controls the church.

The Hireling

The second type of leader Jesus warns about is what we refer to as the *hireling*.

> The hired hand is not the shepherd and does not own the sheep. So when he sees the wolf coming, he abandons the sheep and runs away. Then the wolf attacks the flock and scatters it. The man runs away because he is a hired hand and cares nothing for the sheep. (John 10:12–13)

Jesus says the hired hand is not the rightful guardian or guide of the sheep. Further, Jesus tells us that the *hireling* abandons the sheep because he does not love them. Notice this: the sheep are only a means to the hireling's end—profit and food. In our context, the sheep (meaning the congregation) ultimately mean nothing to the hireling because this type of shepherd takes the job for the money, the attention, the benefits, and the opportunity to move on to bigger sheep pens. They're not in it because they love the people or because they're responsible to the sheep. They forget that the sheep don't follow the shepherd for the good of the shepherd, but because they need direction and care. The hireling has everything exactly backward. The sheep are there for the pastor, they think, not they for the sheep. These pastors see the people as a means to their own glory. It is "my" church and they are "my" people and I am their teacher and "he" is their pastor.

The sign of a hireling is red-faced envy when another voice on the platform draws praise and appreciation, when requests are made for someone else to be given an opportunity to preach. Or when someone mentions to the pastor a book they read and how it transformed their understanding of the Bible or God or Jesus or the church, and the pastor feels compelled to make it clear that author lacks the pastor's approval. These are signs that a pastor is in it for themselves, for their own glory and status. They are a hireling.

Knowing Something's Not Right

If all you've ever known is abusive leadership, how would you know that anything was wrong at all? This is why Jesus says, "I am the good shepherd." He wants his followers to look at how he leads with love, grace, humility, and mercy so they can understand that *these are the marks of what all good leaders should be.* Jesus resets the template for what a leader looks like.

For many people today, deconstruction begins when they see leaders for who they really are. Deconstructors realize they do not see Jesus in their leaders. They witness the use of fear to sell a Jesus who, in reality, continually tells people not to be afraid (Luke 12:7, 32; John 14:27). They hear the hireling saying certain people don't belong in the body of Christ, but they know a Jesus who welcomes everyone to the table (Matthew 9:10–17; Mark 2:13–17; Luke 5:29–39). They hear the hireling issuing harsh judgments and condemnations and acting punitively, while at the same time they recall reading about a Jesus who refuses to condemn, who acts with love instead (John 8:11).

They observe pastors and churches spending exorbitantly on themselves in order to have the best sound systems, musicians, and facilities. The hireling gets to a new location—restaurant, bookstore, speaking event—and immediately begins taking selfies and pictures to post on social media. The hireling wants everyone to know where they are all the time—not because they want accountability, but because they crave attention. All these actions construct a platform for the hireling who wants that platform. The platform is the glory.

When churches present their people with a dichotomy between the Jesus of the Gospels and the platform of the grasper and hireling, they create a moral crisis for the discerning. Their people begin musing, *Something's not right here*, and some eventually make a decision—deconstruct Jesus or deconstruct the hireling and his church and throw out whatever does not belong to Jesus. They are aware that a bevy of bad shepherds are out there, and that bad shepherding causes faith crises. It's what makes them want to reconstruct their faith with Jesus as the Good Shepherd.

A Good Shepherd

Notice again what Jesus says about himself: "I am the good shepherd. The good shepherd lays down his life for the sheep" (John 10:11). These words are a lifeline delivered for the benefit of any leader willing to listen. When Jesus says a good shepherd will give up their life for the sheep, it forces every leader who hears those words to examine their commitment to those they pastor.

Am I willing to put their everyday lives before my own? Am I willing to suffer with them and for them and instead of them?

Jesus presents himself in stark contrast to the leaders standing before him—a dangerous move in that political climate—and challenges them with the question, *Are you willing to be faithful to God's people, even when it gets awful? Are you willing to die for these people? I am.* John 10:11 is a job description for anyone who wants to be a Jesus-like pastor.

A good shepherd is not a grasper or a hireling. A good shepherd is not after power, platform, or money. Their hands are open, holding loosely to whatever authority they have been given. They are never coercive, and they allow people to come and go without condemnation. If you grew up in the evangelical church, perhaps you heard a pastor or visiting missionary tell stories about how shepherds in the ancient world would break the leg of a sheep that kept wandering off in order to protect them. The typical reason for telling a story like this is to communicate that sometimes God will come down harshly on his children, even committing violence or harm to keep someone from walking astray. And at times the grasper or hireling hints that God may be asking them to be his instrument of discipline in the church. If this was something you were taught, then it is likely you have viewed some of the darker times of your life through the lens of "God is breaking my leg because I wandered."

I (Tommy) recently heard those words from an older gentleman at one of our Sunday worship gatherings. He approached me with his wife—a woman with whom I regularly had conversations in the pre-COVID-19 years but whom I hadn't seen much in the years since. She could barely speak. Her brain had been ravaged by Alzheimer's disease, and her husband stood there with tears in his eyes, feeling they were being punished for not being faithful enough. He seemed to feel that his wife's illness was God's public shaming. God was breaking their leg.

These types of stories happen every day in our shame-inducing churches. Hirelings and graspers invariably fail to grasp the depth and width of God's goodness and love. But good shepherds would never hurt sheep in this way, and there is no record of shepherds in either the ancient or modern world breaking a sheep's leg on purpose. Jesus isn't coercive, and he certainly isn't violent.

John 6 records a teaching of Jesus so hard that "many of his disciples turned back and no longer followed him" (6:66). Jesus did not denounce them or insult them. Nor did he turn his back on them. He let them go. He wasn't concerned about drawing huge crowds. Rather, he poured himself out completely for whomever drew near and followed him. Jesus did not tend his Father's sheep for compensation. He loved them to the point of giving up his own reputation and even his life. It's safe to bet he died penniless, for even the clothes he had were cut into pieces and given to the soldiers.

Jesus sets the standards by which God's people will recognize godly leaders who find themselves in positions of power, not enthusiastically, but apprehensively. The power they wield rests in open palms, not in clenched fists. They are sacrificial leaders who mimic Christ, willing to pour themselves out and be broken for the sheep. Dallas Willard once wrote, "Some things that can be pulled cannot be pushed, and some things that can be pushed cannot be pulled. Making disciples is a matter of pulling people."[8] Jesus reveals God as a puller, not a pusher. He goes before us and bids us to come and follow him.

Every few years, I (Tommy) am part of a delegation that votes for a new president for our denomination. Those votes are always preceded by speeches delivered by potential candidates, a plea, if you will, that communicates why they are running for the job and what benefits the people under them will reap. One candidate spoke forcefully about taking the denomination back to its roots, defeating his opponents, and turning back from what he saw as a theological slide away from doctrinally sound positions.

He wrapped up his speech, and the final candidate stepped forward. I was caught off guard by what I heard from him. He stepped forward in a humble posture and spoke softly, without pretense or enthusiasm. He said, "I have no desire to take hold of this position. My hands are open, and God can rest it there for however long he sees fit, or not at all if that's what he desires. I'm just making myself available to whatever God has for me to do." He continued, but instead of talking about himself, he spoke pastorally to the entire denomination: "I want to implore all of you, do not reach for power. If it is for you, God will give it to you. If power and authority are not for you, the worst thing you can do, both for yourself and the church, is to grab hold of it. My hands are open." It was a stark contrast. This is good shepherding, and sheep with this kind of shepherd feel genuinely cared for. Jesus manifests this goodness in his own body, life, and presence.

We wonder what might have happened if deconstructors would have had a spiritual father, like Josh McDowell was to his biological son, who doesn't exercise power *over* people, but understands that the only power they have over someone is expressed in humble service—a leader who has honest, open dialogue while affirming the gifts of others. *That* is how pastors and church leaders can create healthy churches for those who have questions, doubts, and criticisms.

Pastor, are you willing to lay down your power, your image, and even your life, for the sheep? Are you willing to be honest when you don't have an answer? Are you willing to embrace any and every person Jesus brings to you, even at great cost to yourself? Do you pastor the people you have, not the people you want them to be? Jesus did. Deconstructors today speak up and out, sometimes loudly, asking for leaders to lead like the Good Shepherd. Please listen to them.

Toxic leaders need to be purged from the church. If deconstructors would have had a chance to tell us, to have that final exit interview, this is something many would have shared. The question now is, Will we listen? Will they?

11 Trusting Jesus at the Apocalypse

*D*o *you know where you'd go if you were to die right now?*
Do you know where you'd end up in eternity if the rapture occurred today?

Did you just laugh when you read those two questions?

The first two of those questions likely reveal the version of Christianity you grew up with. The third reveals the response of many deconstructors. For most people who were raised in evangelicalism, the answer to those first two questions was once clearer than a crystal sea and shinier than a street paved with gold. There was a time when the average person on the street thought about such things, when they believed there was more to life than what they saw with their eyes. It was a time when you could have a conversation about this with a well-meaning stranger. I (Tommy) know because I used to do it—it was once called open-air evangelism, which is now so out of step with modern culture that videos of open-air evangelists now appear in social media feeds next to videos of car crashes and screaming Karens.

I left home for Bible college at the age of seventeen, and every student was required to take part in at least four evangelistic outings every year. The school van would drop us off in an area of Tampa called Ybor City, a bit like the French Quarter in New Orleans but less Creole and more Cuban. It was the party strip, and we were out there in our button-down shirts, well-versed in our gimmicks but still trying to get people saved. By *gimmicks*, I am referring to the different ways we were taught to strike up a conversation or attract an audience. A few students carried magic rope tricks, while others carried something called the EvangeCube (I don't want to explain this one; just google it). We also had the "wordless book"—a book designed with blank sheets of different colored construction paper to assist us as we told the story of Jesus. Of course, it also had a white page representing goodness and a black page representing badness and sin (obviously problematic). I still cringe thinking about all this twenty-five years later.

One of the guys in the van with us was a painter. He could tell the story of Jesus while standing on the corner with his easel and paint a pretty decent-looking portrayal of the crucifixion. Others of us with no talent were instructed to dress casually and pretend to be part of the gathered crowd, enamored and hanging on every word. This act was meant to help gather a *real* crowd of unsuspecting pub crawlers who were about to be confronted with the eternal damnation of their soul.

As embarrassing as the whole thing is, when I look back to the 1990s, people were generally still open to talking about death and whatever lies beyond, especially if it involved religion and the state of our souls. But as we moved into a new century with new ways of gathering information via the internet, we had new ways of processing this information and fact-checking it. It became easier to compare an idea with Christian thinkers down through the centuries, to tool around the internet searching for other opinions. Things changed.

Deconstructors don't accept easy answers to those questions any longer, and they challenge the premise of the question itself. Answers now have less certainty and more nuance. The challenges they offer became questions like these:

- What is heaven, after all?
- Do only evangelicals go to heaven? (Plus a few other lucky ones?)
- What did the first-century Jews like Jesus and the apostles believe about death and what lay beyond it?
- Did they all believe the same thing?
- Why do some evangelical beliefs seem more platonic (the soul leaving the body) than others (the body and the soul remain inseparable)?
- And doesn't the New Testament say something about heaven coming to earth instead of the opposite—earth coming to heaven?
- And what's the rapture all about? Do people still believe in it?

Many pastors watched as a wave of deconstruction washed over cherished Christian beliefs about heaven and hell—ideas so cherished they were the foundation of the questions asked at the start of this chapter. At first it was a few edgier books, mostly pointing out disagreements on the topic throughout church history, books such as Rob Bell's *Love Wins* and Brian D. McLaren's *The Last Word and The Word After That*. These books quickly got their authors pushed off the platforms of evangelical institutions. Consider the words of John Piper, who famously issued his anathema via a three-word tweet: "Farewell Rob Bell" (@JohnPiper, February 26, 2011). But ejecting Rob Bell from the conversation didn't silence his readers. Nor did those ejections stop deconstructors from asking more questions.

Instead of acknowledging the difficulties of knowing about our postmortem fate, the powers in the evangelical church spoke loudly against questioning cherished beliefs. Others doubled down by saying that *insiders* go to heaven and *outsiders* go to hell. By *heaven* they typically meant a place far away from this drab earth where everything is perfect and no tears are ever cried again. And by *hell* they meant eternal conscious torment— constant and never-ceasing torture on repeat twenty-four hours a day, forever and ever.

What happens when the hell leg, if not two hell legs, are knocked out from the stool that evangelicalism is sitting on? What happens to the gospel when hell isn't what they think it is? Hell is one of the most persistent and problematic topics among deconstructors as they deconstruct. Why, they ask, does God (or the church) have to motivate a right response to the gospel by the fear of eternal conscious torment? Doesn't the darling verse of evangelicalism begin with "For God so loved the world" (John 3:16)? Yes, it does. Then why does their opening to the gospel sound more like "For God so hates you?" Yes, why?

The personal stories we've heard from and about deconstructors and their experience with what pastors and parents teach about hell is painful to read, but we offer a few snapshots from one of Scot's previous books to highlight the personal impact this cherished Christian idea has had on some:

> Belief in hell has led some to contend the Christian faith is inherently unjust and morally repugnant. On top of that there lies the inevitable question of how God can justly punish eternally billions of humans who have never heard about God's grace in Jesus Christ, or who have barely heard, or who have literally been banned from hearing? The prospect of holding onto an orthodox doctrine of hell after one wades through this ugly ditch has led some to leave the Christian faith or an orthodox version of that faith.

> Quoting Julie Bogart: "Hell is such a damned long time and yet so many people throw it all into the big mystery box: God is just, it's a mystery. My response: what you believe about that question determines how you live your life. Therefore, we're compelled to come to conclusions about heaven and hell. It can't remain a mystery. . . . So the quest to understand the definitive answer about salvation and the lost is what led to the theological reading which began the unraveling process."

> Paraphrasing Charles Templeton: "The idea of an endless hell is a monstrous concept. That a so-called loving Father would condemn his children—no matter how persistently obdurate—to be tortured forever, with no hope for a reprieve, is barbarous beyond belief and can only be dismissed as ancient sadistic nonsense."[1]

The rush to silence deconstructors' questions about universalism, annihilationism, and other alternative ideas has often led to heated confrontations. Some churches fired pastors. Others split over the question of whether or not the God revealed by Jesus Christ would send someone to suffer eternal conscious torment. Someone we know hid his copy of *Love Wins* inside the dust jacket of a John Piper book so he could read it at his Christian university without being chastised.

The controversy has endured because, while we ask a lot of questions about what the Bible says, we rarely ask *the* question we've been encouraging you throughout this book to ask: *Is this belief Christlike? Is what we believe God will do in the end something true to the nature of Jesus Christ?* And we also need to ask a few follow-up questions: "Can I *trust* Jesus? Can I trust him with aging parents, with terminally ill friends, with those in our lives we love and worry about? Can we trust Jesus to catch them with love, to judge them in love, and to love them in our absence?"

Let's pause here and sit with these questions as we turn to Jesus' words on death and resurrection. As we do, here's another question to consider: *What happens to the way we talk about heaven and hell when these words of Jesus are the guiding words for the discussion?*

Easter Day Gospel

A common motif found in ancient portrayals of the crucifixion in media or art depicts Jesus rising from the tomb, surrounded by his family and his disciples. Many of these works of art also contain the image of Jesus rising from the tomb while holding the hand of two other people. With his right hand, Jesus lifts a fallen man from the earth, and with his left hand, he clenches a woman's hand as he lifts her from the ground. The man and woman represent Adam and Eve, and they are rising with Jesus from their graves, finding their true final destiny in the resurrection of Jesus.[2]

In the background of icons of the Orthodox Church are two additional symbols: jagged rocks that signal the event's historicity and an almond-shaped doorway, called the mandorla, emphasizing the resurrection's spiritual meaning. When we see these symbols together, we're being told that the event depicted is both historical *and* spiritual. For Christians throughout history, the resurrection of Christ was more than just an event with locations, names, and facts; it was a message to be proclaimed, one with importance for all of humanity.

In the evangelical tradition, beliefs about the resurrection are often shallower than a shallow grave. This is because most evangelicals see the cross as the center of Jesus' work. I (Scot) often call this the "Good Friday gospel." Children in Sunday school sing songs about Jesus being "born to die" and about our hope being "built on nothing less than Jesus' blood and righteousness." Most grew up singing with gusto about "the old rugged cross."

What's the cultural deposit here? The resurrection becomes an afterthought. Sadly, it's nothing more than a happy ending to a sorrowful story about a wonderful man named Jesus. It's the ten-second clip at the end of Mel Gibson's *The Passion of the Christ* or the M. Night Shyamalan twist as the finale of an otherwise-horrific ending. This Good Friday gospel leads many deconstructors to ask, "Does the resurrection matter for the gospel?" Other than going to heaven when we die, which is no small matter to be sure, is there an "Easter Day gospel"?

The Good Friday gospel story teaches young Christians to believe that each of us was born losing the ultimate game. The point of life is to figure out how to win the game and get to heaven when you die. Once you figure out the winning strategy—that the solution is, *Jesus died for my sins*—your job now becomes trying to convince others of the correct solution so they, too, can go to heaven. If the entire aim of Christianity is going to heaven after we die, we will all too easily fall into an escapist lifestyle that does not much care about making things right in the world. If the ultimate goal is the afterlife, let the world burn.

A faith shaped by the ultimate aim of leaving this world and going to heaven, whether at the rapture or at death, is blind to social crises. A majority of White evangelicals in America have never experienced any type of government oppression and have no memory of what bondage under power feels like. For the most part, White evangelicals have comfortably theorized over cool drinks on cushioned couches about the meaning of life, heaven and hell, and where we go when we die. For them, heaven and hell are not about now; they are about later—and the later the better.

But for our Black, Latin, Indigenous, and Asian brothers and sisters in the church, the experience of history has been different. For many historically oppressed people, resurrection is about Jesus' descent into the darkest of hells—hells they may be all too familiar with—and rescuing Adam and Eve, his humanity, his *imago Dei*. It is about liberation from oppression, slavery, and systemic injustices. Resurrection raises them up from darkness to join a great cloud of witnesses. The resurrection of the crucified Jesus has become for them a message of hope for a world made right again.

They know Good Friday already—every day. What they want is Easter. They plead with God for Easter to break out in their lives, their communities, and their nations. Easter conquers the grave and liberates the occupied. Our oppressed brothers and sisters, like Jesus in his uplift, discover others in their hands. "Come along," they say. "Jesus is right here with us. He's got us in his hands, and we've got you. Come along."

Resurrection Is a Promise

In April 2023, an African American lawmaker in the state of Tennessee was voted out for violating rules of decorum. He and two other lawmakers had joined a protest against guns, and the state legislature voted to remove him and one other African American male. Another legislator, a White woman, barely survived the vote and remained in the legislature. Guns were their concern, but our concern is primarily with was what was said from the floor by one of the ousted lawmakers, Justin J. Pearson. His message, given during Holy Week, was a call to march right through the final week of Jesus—his goodness, his protests, his rejection, his arrest, his unjust crucifixion—and on to its fitting completion on Easter morning when God suffocated death and raised Jesus from the dead.

The resurrection of Jesus gave Justin J. Pearson hope for justice, for turning around Tennessee's violence against children in a Christian school to make the state a safer place for all people. Resurrection, for Justin J. Pearson, was not about what happens when he dies, but about what can happen now because the new creation was launched on Easter morning. In his words:

> I remember on Friday that my Savior Jesus—a man who was innocent of all crimes except fighting for the poor, fighting

for the marginalized, fighting for the LGBTQ community, fighting for those who are single mothers, fighting for those who are ostracized, and fighting for those pushed to the periphery—my Savior, my Black Jesus, he was lynched by the government on Friday, and they thought that all hope had been lost. Oh, on the outside it rained and it thundered and everybody said everything was over. And, it was some Black women who stood at the cross, it was some Black women who watched what the government did to that boy named Jesus. There were witnesses, as you have been witnesses to what is happening in the anti-democratic state of Tennessee. There were witnesses to what was going on, and I gotta tell you it got quiet on Saturday. Yes, I tell you it was a sad day on Saturday. All hope seemed to be lost.

Representatives were thrown out of the State House. Democracy seemed to be at its end, seemed like the NRA and gun lobbyists might win. But all that was good news for us. I don't know how long this Saturday in the state of Tennessee might last, but, oh, we have good news, folks. We've got good news that Sunday always comes. Resurrection is a promise, and it is a prophecy. It's a prophecy that came out of the cotton fields. It's a prophecy that came out of the lynching tree. It's a prophecy that still lives in each and every one of us in order to make the state of Tennessee the place that it ought to be. So I've still got hope because I know we are still here, and we will never quit.[3]

"Out of order," said the judge, and we heard the sound of the gavel. The resurrection sermon to the state of Tennessee was over.

When our minority sisters and brothers work for resurrection in their own communities, they are often called left-wing political extremists. Their sermons are picked apart, their earnestness is questioned, and their hope is diminished. A 2022 HarperCollins study found that significantly more deconstructors who changed their beliefs are located among the more ethnically diverse.[4] A faith structure that sees social justice and equality as "polishing brass on the *Titanic*" is of no use to the current generation. Either the gospel flows out of Good Friday and Easter, or it is no gospel at all.

The ethnically non-White are highly connected to friends around the globe. They are keenly aware of systemic injustice. They are not interested in a Jesus who offers nothing to the suffering, the oppressed, and the marginalized. They want a life worth living *now* that derives from a Jesus who unleashes abundant life in the here and now. They are looking for a Jesus who gives them life *before* death, not just after death.

Resurrection Life

If there was meaning beyond the tragic events of the death of Jesus, *and if* Easter morning was supposed to provide us with a living hope in the here and now, many of us grew up completely unaware of it. We grew up with a Good Friday gospel. We only sang "up from the grave he arose" once a year. In fact, this one-sided and, if we are being honest, lazy and half-baked telling of the gospel story left us unempowered to participate in the mission of the church. Is resurrection, many today are asking, *really* all about the afterlife? Did God really create the entire universe, guide Israel's entire history, enter the world, and live for three hard decades only to be tortured and killed just so humans could scoot to heaven when they die?

Jesus predicted not only his horrific death but also his

glorious resurrection (Mark 8:31; 9:31; 10:34), and the apostles preached a resurrection gospel (Acts 2:32; Romans 1:4). In the crack of a tomb, God turned injustice into justice when crucifixion became resurrection.

Notice these early church proclamations: "For one of these must become a witness with us of his resurrection"; "they were . . . proclaiming in Jesus the resurrection of the dead"; and "With great power the apostles continued to testify to the resurrection of the Lord Jesus" (Acts 1:22; 4:2, 33). Until Good Friday becomes Easter morn, it is not the gospel. Good Friday turns evil into good through resurrection.

For the early church, the resurrection signaled a new epoch. Those earliest followers of Jesus believed that something in the universe had fundamentally changed at the resurrection of Christ. His resurrection turned a gruesome death into atonement. Easter gave them hope and courage to tell the world about Jesus, endure intense persecution, and continue on as followers of Jesus, loving their enemies, serving the poor, and welcoming outsiders. What is being taught about the resurrection of Jesus in present-day evangelicalism does not seem to have the same effect that the message of resurrection did in the early church. It does not draw hope out of us or give us a picture of what Jesus can do for our world or our neighborhoods, and it offers us little more than heaven when we die (which is no small gift). We have sold the gospel short because we have stopped with a gruesome death midday on Good Friday.

The Resurrection of Lazarus

Resurrection was God's design all along. Not death, but life. The last word God speaks is life. Which was why Jesus went face-to-face with a hopeless friend in John 10. He looked into her reddened, tear-soaked eyes and said, "I am the resurrection and the life" (John 11:25). Jesus' terse self-claim was not a tactless pastoral word of consolation for a grieving sister. With that "I Am" claim, Jesus provided for Martha a stunning worldview.

You see, Jesus had just received word that his friend Lazarus was sick. Lazarus lived in Bethany of Judea with his sisters, Mary and Martha. Jesus had a close relationship with this small family. When Jesus heard that Lazarus was sick, he reassured those gathered around him that "this sickness will not end in death" (11:4).

Clearly in no hurry, Jesus stayed where he was for two more days, and then he and his disciples made the journey. Upon their arrival, they discovered that Lazarus had been dead for four days. (He was apparently already dead when Jesus had first heard the news of Lazarus's sickness.) Verses 20 through 26 tell us what happened when Jesus showed up.

> When Martha heard that Jesus was coming, she went out to meet him, but Mary stayed at home.
>
> "Lord," Martha said to Jesus, "if you had been here, my brother would not have died. But I know that even now God will give you whatever you ask."
>
> Jesus said to her, "Your brother will rise again."
>
> Martha answered, "I know he will rise again in the resurrection at the last day."
>
> Jesus said to her, "I am the resurrection and the life. The one who believes in me will live, even though they die; and whoever lives by believing in me will never die. Do you believe this?"

John tells us that Jesus then went with them to the tomb of Lazarus, accompanied by other Jewish neighbors and friends who were there to mourn with them and comfort them. But when they arrived, life cracked open the grave of death. Jesus said to remove the stone from the entrance of the cave in which he was buried, but the sisters replied (verses 39–44):

> "But, Lord," said Martha, the sister of the dead man, "by this time there is a bad odor, for he has been there four days."
>
> Then Jesus said, "Did I not tell you that if you believe, you will see the glory of God?"
>
> So they took away the stone. Then Jesus looked up and said, "Father, I thank you that you have heard me. I knew that you always hear me, but I said this for the benefit of the people standing here, that they may believe that you sent me."
>
> When he had said this, Jesus called in a loud voice, "Lazarus, come out!" The dead man came out, his hands and feet wrapped with strips of linen, and a cloth around his face.
>
> Jesus said to them, "Take off the grave clothes and let him go."

Believe it or not, resurrection—that is, the restoration of a body after death—was not a popular idea outside of Judaism in the first century. The very suggestion of human bodies being reanimated would have offended the sensibilities of especially the Greek intellectuals of Jesus' day. They held a low view of the human body, seeing it more as a container for the soul than something God purposefully called "good." To them, the *body* wasn't much more than the brown box from Amazon that arrives on your doorstep and is quickly thrown out once the item inside is removed. *The content of the body*—the soul—is what was important in their view. And yet it seems that most Jewish people in the world of Jesus believed in resurrection,[5] that is, the general resurrection (especially of law-abiding Jews).

Martha believed in the resurrection. She had just confessed as much to Jesus. For Martha, though, the resurrection would come later, at the end of all things, in what she called "the last day" (John 11:24). For Martha, whose beliefs in some ways parallel many Christians today, resurrection was a God-thing for the future, not a God-act in the present. She was about to learn something wild.

Deconstructors are wearied by a Good Friday gospel that never gets to Sunday's Easter gospel. They are tired of atonement theology that does nothing more than wipe away a debt or forgive sins. They long for the expansive and empowering grace that deals death to sin but then explodes into a life that brings healing for one's family, one's friends, one's church, one's community, and the world. Their eyes light up when the resurrection gospel flows out of the crucifixion gospel. They don't want Martha's general-resurrection hope; they want the graveclothes off and the dead man walking.

The Good News of the Last Day

In synagogue, Martha heard about the last day, or the day of the Lord. That day was more than just a day of general resurrection for God's people. On that day, the Lord would establish peace in the world and all wrongs would be made right. Most importantly, it was a day when Roman oppression over Judea would end.

And, as John the Baptist's father sang, it would be a day when the people of God would experience:

"salvation from our enemies
and from the hand of all who hate us."

A day on which God would arise:

"to show mercy to our ancestors
and to remember his holy covenant,
the oath he swore to our father Abraham."
(Luke 1:71–73)

But the day of the Lord was more than a display of God's faithfulness to the covenant with Abraham. Yes, it would be a display of God's faithfulness, but God's faithfulness also meant a day on which God would show up:

"to rescue us from the hand of our enemies,
and to enable us to serve him without fear
in holiness and righteousness before him all
our days." (Luke 1:74–75)

It would be the day of covenant, social, political, and spiritual redemption. The evangelical church, when taken in a wide sweep, has neglected social liberation and justice and peace as the heart of the gospel's redemption. Nothing disappoints deconstructors more than to hear the gospel is a "first things first" gospel—first spiritual redemption and then social liberation. But the gospel is *simultaneously* salt and light, spiritual and social, internal and external.

Deconstructors know that those who opt for the "first things first" gospel almost never get to the social dimensions of the gospel. Deconstructors despise choosing between a spiritual and social gospel. They believe the spiritual gospel is social; they believe the social gospel is spiritual. And this double gospel of redemption—the crucifixion plus the resurrection, the spiritual and the social—should be a living reality in the church, but they don't see that happening. They urge the "first things first" church to get this right in its own life before becoming political actors. When the church finally gets the double gospel right, they will become witnesses of what happens when the day of the Lord breaks into the present world.

Unfortunately, many today speak of the day of the Lord as if it was a terrible event, a day of fear and trembling. I (Tommy) came of age in a stream of Christianity that taught a bleak view of that day. I believed the day of the Lord would come at the end of a long and terrible time when God, full of wrath and anger, would spew out judgment on the whole earth. In that day, there would be famine and war, culminating in a violent and bloody battle led by a sword-wielding Jesus riding a white horse while slaying his enemies.

Many have called this day the Battle of Armageddon. But I have since come to agree with the first-century folks who saw the day of the Lord as a great day of hope for all humanity, a day when the world would be made right and a good king—the promised King and Messiah—would sit on the throne of the universe to establish God's final rule of peace and justice. All debts would be erased and all sins forgiven, and humanity, having found its place under God's reign, would finally reach the fullness of its identity in God.

New Testament scholar Timothy Gombis writes that in the future age Israel was waiting for, "all of God's people would

experience the overwhelming blessings of the land's flourishing and productivity, and all of creation would be renewed."[6]
Resurrection was much bigger than the reanimation of a few
bodies. Martha was about to learn that, for Jesus, resurrection
launched not just hope for the future but a new creation for this
world.

Deconstructors are unlearning the terrifying view of the
future they inherited. Many were saddled with a theology that
gave them persistent anxiety, worried they might be *left behind*
and that their parents and siblings would disappear in the middle
of the night and they'd be all alone in a world that would end in
horrific violence. Worse yet, they were taught that this was God's
best plan for the world, that a good God had somehow planned
out a future of blood, starvation, pain, and misery for them.
These things are not just hard to unlearn; they have to be shaken
from our bones.

Many who begin to deconstruct the politics of the church
in which they were raised realize that much of what they were
taught was based on speculative interpretations of books like
Revelation. Their support for Israel and their hatred for Palestine,
avid support for (mostly) unregulated gun ownership, anti-
environmentalism, and other items on a political platform can be
traced back to their *eschatology*—their understanding of the end-
times. Many have been led to believe that theological ideas like
the rapture are cornerstones of the ancient Christian faith when,
in reality, most of the ideas in this speculative approach to the
world's future are less than two hundred years old. When deconstructors realize they've been duped into anticreation political
positions based on a superficial theology, it becomes hard to earn
their trust again.

This is precisely why the I Am statements of Jesus are a helpful guide for skeptics, doubters, Nones, and Dones. The I Ams lead us into a new Garden of Eden with Jesus. Jesus said he is the resurrection. So when the church talks about the end times, and church leaders purport to know God's plans for the end, we are to judge it all against Christ. Is that future *Christlike*? Or does it sound like it came from a foreign policy memo written by a government official in the military offices of the Pentagon? Does this depiction of God's plan for the future sound like the One who is the resurrection and the life? Or does it all sound too *them-like* and not enough *Christlike*? If Jesus is, as Paul writes in 1 Corinthians 15:20, "the firstfruits of those who have fallen asleep," then we must look to *Jesus* to understand God's future.

12 Discerning Jesus as the Way

Leena grew up in a devout evangelical family. She was taught from a young age that following a strict set of rules and beliefs was the only way to please God and guarantee her salvation. The house rules were clear and nonnegotiable and many of them seemed pointlessly gender-specific. For years, she found comfort in a clear sense of order. Order bred a feeling of certainty and security. But as she grew older, she felt increasingly skeptical of the rules and expectations of her faith community. She felt like she was constantly scrutinized and judged by those around her, and she struggled to reconcile the rigid, insider-versus-outsider worldview of evangelicalism with the complex realities of life.

Eventually, Leena began to read books and listen to podcasts by those who felt as she did about the church—that it was a place of ostracism rather than embrace. She was beginning to find that many other people shared her doubts and questions. Over time, her faith changed. It became more nuanced, complex, and complicated. She learned there were many different Christian traditions, often marked by stark differences about what God asks of the Christian life. She experienced what pastor Adam Hamilton described in his book *Seeing Gray in a World of Black and White*.[1] Her own black-and-white world, with its clear order and certain distinctions, had become gray.

If there are Christians all over the world who disagree on various moral issues, some of great importance, then how, she was asking, are we to understand the Christian life? Do we follow the Old Testament law? Do we simply follow the Ten Commandments? Do we make a list of dos and don'ts from Paul's letters? All of these questions are relevant and necessary because, in case you haven't been paying attention, the ethics of the American church are in a bad place, not just among congregants, but among leadership as well.

To make it worse, whenever a church leader does something wildly immoral, there are always defenders who argue that their behavior wasn't so bad. And when deconstructors hear others saying that pastoral abuse, sexual or otherwise, only reveals that we are all sinners, the doors swing open and the disillusioned leave, some never to return. If church leaders aren't examples of following Jesus, of good morality, then why bother?

I (Tommy) once heard one of my seminary professors describe the Torah as a "finger-pointing." The Torah is the Old Testament body of laws given to Israel by Moses—a collection of 613 of them. The Israelites believed the Torah was a gift God gave as a guide to help them fulfill their mission in God's plan. The Law was "the way." At least for some.

The Torah was the Israelites' path in this world, and they believed it would lead to a flourishing life. But it proved to be difficult at times. There was the daily struggle to observe the law and remain clean, the trudging forward by priests in Jerusalem who attended to the daily sacrifices and prayers. And there were groups badgering one another over how to live the holiest life.

Each of these various religious groups of the time promised a better future— the Essenes, the Pharisees, the Sadducees, and the Zealots. (For our purposes here, we are ignoring the in-betweens, eclectics, and—hardest of all to pin down—ordinary Jews who lived good Jewish lives.) Of these four, the Essenes went radical for holiness and separation from all that didn't meet their interpretations of the Torah. They were so radical that at least some of them moved out to form a desert community near the Dead Sea—a very tough place to live. The Pharisees were the more liberal or progressive of these groups who did their best to adjust the Torah to the times in which they lived so that more and more people could be observant. The Sadducees were the aristocratic establishment who saw a future for Israel if it stayed true to the temple and its priests. The Zealots grew weary of both the Pharisees and Sadducees and said, "Our future is in our hands. Pick up a sword, and let's go to war and kick the Romans out of the land."

It's not difficult to think of various groups in our world today that adopt differing approaches, much like these groups. Each possessed deep convictions about the right path for all Israelites to experience God's blessing. Each group was as certain of what they believed as Charles Darwin's successors are of naturalistic evolution.

Every denomination today has historical roots, and for the most part, they all began with the certainty that they possessed the sure and living way for the church. The more or less unified, "small *c*" catholic church gave way to the Eastern Orthodox and Western Roman Catholic Church. Centuries later, Roman Catholics gave way to Protestants, who themselves split into Lutherans and Reformed, and eventually into Anabaptists as well. Those Protestants then broke into an English group we call the Church of England, or Anglicans, which spawned the Presbyterians and the Congregationalists and the Baptists. So began what we now call "denominations." And while this simplistic sketch skips over many groups, our point is that all of the various shapes and directions offered *not just a theology, but the best way to live the Christian life.*

So which groups have the truth? Deconstructors ask, "Do any of them have the full truth?" and then, "Does it matter?" For most of them, the answer to both of those questions is no. Certainty in such matters is unattainable.[2]

The Way

Many young evangelicals view the American church with the same confusion. With their mouths, church leaders say, "Salvation is by grace through faith," but their actual behaviors and postures speak otherwise. Instead of a life of grace, their lives say, *Our rules are the way, our politics are the way, our economic model is the way, our view of the family is the way*, and on and on in an endless expansion of the one true way. And like every other group, they move as carefully as they can through their day trying to walk the way. It's all black and white for each group. The only shades of gray are about the matters that don't matter. Until they do.

Certainty and fundamentalism are tied together at the head, waist, and ankle. Fundamentalism is shaped by rules, with many who were raised in fundamentalism still living with a subtle, constant feeling of doom. One does not shed one's fundamentalist conscience with a baptism or a shift in denominations. Former fundies will still laugh with one another about some rule they grew up with—like not going to a movie, abstaining from alcohol, or refusing to attend a wedding at a Catholic church— but they'll long remember the effects of the socialization they received from their parents, churches, and pastors. The rules of their youth shaped them and continue to shape them. They were firm and sure.

Deconstructors frequently walk out the door of these rule-shaped churches. More often than not, they leave because they choose to live, not by rules, but in the way mapped by Jesus. When Jesus said, "I am the way" (John 14:6), he offered to his disciples a new, fresh way to live a flourishing life. The old way was given to them through Moses, but Jesus positioned himself as a new and improved Moses, a Moses 2.0. Jesus both formed a new group—a kingdom coalition—and called people away from other groups.

If Jesus is the Way, then all that is required is to follow him. He walked the road ahead of both the committed and the curious. He offered them a life lived in wisdom and humility. He showed them how to love their enemies, how to be led by the Holy Spirit, and how to shun the power (might) of the world for God's power (which is displayed in weakness). He revealed a God who poured out power on people so they could live in a way that mirrored the cross—doing acts of sacrifice, showing mercy, practicing humility, working on righteousness, and lavishing love on everyone they encounter.

Following Jesus entirely transforms what it means to live the good life. Following a person cannot be reduced to following a set of rules. The Way transcends a doctrine to affirm and a rule book to follow. The Way is a person. The Way is Jesus. His way is how he understands and teaches the Torah. Jesus surely challenges the other ways the disciples had known. They had been told for so long that the true way was to follow the Torah of Moses. That true way, of course, involved an interpretation—whether they should adopt the Pharisee way, the Essene way, the Zealot way, or the Sadducee way. There was no Torah of Moses that was not also an interpretation of the Torah of Moses.

But Jesus challenged all of those ways with a new way. Jesus did not "come to abolish the Law or the Prophets; I have not come to abolish them but to fulfill them" (Matthew 5:17). That is, he offered a challenge to the other groups with a fresh reading of the Torah. Jesus centered his reading of the Torah in (1) loving God and (2) loving others. Everything he did and taught worked its way out from those two principal commands.

As we read the Gospels, we observe Jesus at the table with people deemed *sinners*. "Sinners," at least according to those who gave Jesus a hard time, was code language for "do not follow our interpretation of the Torah." But Jesus offered a different interpretation, one rooted in the command to love God and love others. He loved sinners in ways that brought healing, comfort, repentance, righteousness, and inclusion. That was his way.

Most deconstructors leave in order to follow the Way, and at the very least, the dimensions of the Way we discuss next are most attractive to them. Over and over we have observed that deconstructors are not walking out the church doors to enter a life of sin. Rather, statistics show they want a more Jesus-centered religion.

An Inclusive Way

It's easy to get lost in squishy thinking about Jesus. Why? Because each of us—repeat this—each of us thinks we are following the Way. Researchers once did a personality survey of public school students in the UK (a study we referenced in chapter 4). As you may recall, the test was simple—two dozen questions about their own personality, and the same two dozen questions adjusted only slightly to talk about Jesus.

Are you an introvert? Was Jesus an introvert?

It's a clever set of questions. The test measured up to the standards for reliable tests, and the results were beyond clever. In fact, they were stunning in two ways. First, everyone correlated the answers about their own personality to the personality of Jesus. And second, most of the students taking the test were not Christians or even church attenders. But Christian or not, most wanted Jesus on their side. Christian or not, most thought they were like Jesus (or Jesus was like them). We bring this up to make one observation: *Everyone does the same thing. We all like to think we are like Jesus.* The problem this test reveals is that *we make Jesus more like us than we are like Jesus.* That's what we mean when we say we must avoid being squishy.

What is not squishy is that Jesus attracted crowds of people. Mix into that nonsquishy observation the reality that some of those attracted to him were the marginalized, sinful, nonobservant, and demonized. Jesus' inclusiveness of *all*—and here we avoid the squishy—meant they would need to watch and listen to Jesus and learn to walk with him and his kingdom coalition.

To help us do the same, we offer some open-ended, "whoever wants to follow me can" statements of Jesus:

> Therefore whoever hears these words of mine and puts them
> into practice is like a wise man who built his house on the rock.
> (Matthew 7:24, author's translation)

> For whoever does the will of my Father in heaven is my brother
> and sister and mother. (Matthew 12:50)

> Therefore, whoever takes the lowly position of this child is the
> greatest in the kingdom of heaven. (Matthew 18:4)

It does not matter who it is. Who*ever* wants to follow the
Way can. And Jesus knows who follows him and who does not.
Those who put his words into practice, those who do the will of
his Father, and those who choose the path of humility and non-
celebrity. Who*ever*. These are the ones on the path with Jesus.

Jesus' way is not exclusionary. He was not sent into the world "to
condemn the world, but to save the world through him" (John 3:17).
Jesus says much the same about himself when he told his listeners,
"I did not come to judge the world, but to save the world" (12:47).
Earlier we observed that many people begin their life with God
thinking that he hates them because they are sinners. That disposi-
tion fails the Jesus test. Jesus did not come to judge or to condemn;
he came to save. Because God "loves the world so much he sent Jesus
to the world" (3:16, author's translation), Jesus' way is inclusionary.
God loves everyone. Jesus loves everyone. To everyone, he is offering
a warm welcome and sincere invitation to follow the Way.

The "insider versus outsider" and the "our way versus all
other ways" are not the ways of Jesus. Okay, we'll say it: Jesus
said his way was *easy*! Here are his words: "Come to me, all you
who are weary and burdened, and I will give you rest. Take my

yoke upon you and learn from me, for I am gentle and humble in heart, and you will find rest for your souls. For my yoke is easy and my burden is light" (Matthew 11:28–30).

His yoke is easy because his approach to people is to give them grace, to empower them, to walk with them, to offer others to be their companions on the way, to provide nourishment, to raise them up when they fall, and to instruct them all along the way.

Some profoundly exclusionary ways in the church have turned off deconstructors and disillusioned them. Strict rules not taught by Jesus exclude. Economic class excludes. Theological systems exclude. Ageism excludes. Ableism excludes. Genderism excludes. Cultural clout excludes. Power excludes. Education excludes. Racism excludes.

Consider this observation by Jeff Liou, who is the national director of theological formation for InterVarsity Christian Fellowship:

> Having worked in campus ministry since 2001, I have not seen the kind of exodus of young people of color from the church like I have seen since 2016. One group informed me that their church's failure to speak meaningfully after the police killings of black men was a kind of color blindness that disillusioned and dismayed them. Numerous groups of college students in the most diverse generations to date define themselves in opposition to white evangelicalism on more topics than just race. The work of " deconstruction" has led many young people to scrutinize the assumptions of traditional, Western doctrines [like original sin]. I have also listened as Christian leaders have contemptuously dismissed this deconstruction. They are unable to perceive the seriousness of the chasm that separates them from people they might otherwise serve.[3]

Deconstructors practice nuance rather than exclusionary thinking. Increasingly, they perceive racism behind many of the current forms of exclusion and show finesse in tying race, economics, power, and Christian theology into a bundle of exclusion. They are looking for the Jesus who snaps the knots so he can knit those cords into opportunities of inclusion and unity instead. If they must leave the exclusionary church to find the inclusionary Jesus and his kingdom coalition, they will. And they have.

A Truthful Way

As moderns and postmoderns, we have a troubled relationship with truth. Many believed the information age would sort out our struggles to understand each other and the world around us. With data-packed computers in our pockets, we thought we would know and be known. We would finally understand what was happening in the world around us, why it was happening, and how we might right the wrongs of society. We would finally know *the truth*. We weren't naïve, but we were hopeful. Much of this confidence and certainty was unconscious. Our TV shows shifted from *The Flintstones* to *The Jetsons* who lived in Orbit City. Robots were everywhere because everything could be figured out. All it would take was more information, more knowledge.

It turns out that truth is more complicated than possessing more data and information. In the postmodern absence of an agreed-on truth source—a metanarrative or story that pulls all the data into a coherent meaning—influential people manipulate data to serve their own power-filled purposes. They invent ways to misinterpret, misinform, and bend true information to fit preconceived narratives that align with what their followers want to believe about themselves and the world around them.

The irony of our age is that though we have more information and greater access to data, we are more suspicious of that information and more deceitful in how we use it. We no longer trust email requests from our bank or Amazon because they might be phishing attempts or embezzlement attacks. Businesses now have massive budgets to ward off hackers and poachers. Living in the abundance of the information age, we have witnessed the erosion of trust.

Over the summer of 2020, many churchgoers, confined to their homes because of the COVID-19 pandemic, spent inordinate amounts of time on the internet looking for answers, hope, connection—any kind of information that would help them make it to tomorrow. During this same time, we saw church folks of all stripes gleefully sharing what we now call "misinformation," a politically gentle way of saying *lies*. Some was spread to tarnish the names of elected officials and government workers who did not share their ideological viewpoints. From the same mouths came both adoring sermons about Jesus and misinformation about a pandemic that has, as of February 2023, killed more than 7.3 million people worldwide.[4]

Hypocrisy sparks deconstruction. If people can't trust us to tell the truth about something as serious as a pandemic and how to protect ourselves, then if they witness blatant lies, how can they trust what we say about God? How can we know someone isn't sharing disinformation about God? How do we know if a trusted leader hasn't been doing that for years?

Sadly, many pastors are willing to ignore an attribute or two, a doctrine or two, or a practice or two of Jesus when it doesn't support their ideological narrative. Where are people in a postmodern world supposed to find truth when those who claim to

disseminate the truth are themselves disposed to disinformation and conspiracy theories? We all need a truth awakening, a
cultural revolution in which truth becomes a prized, disciplined
value. And many deconstructors are turning to Jesus, the Way,
to find the truth.

A Personal Way

The ancient world had its own struggles with truth. There was
plenty of debate about the character of God, the desires of God,
and the role of God's people in this world. Some thought the
people of God were still in exile, even though they were living
in their promised land—that is, they believed the Roman occupation was defiling the land and kept them from being truly at
home. Some reasoned that if sin had led to exile, then *holiness*
would end the exile. They believed renewed covenant faithfulness
was the way to restoration. The basic theology for such persons
was sin → exile → return/restoration. This narrative told the
story of everything, explaining Israel's past, present, and future.

Jesus entered into this pattern of thinking with a challenge
like none other. Yes, God gave the Torah, and the Torah was
Israel's special privilege. But the way to read the Torah and to
understand its message, Jesus proposed, was like this: "No one
comes to the Father except through me. If you really know me,
you will know my Father as well. From now on, you do know him
and have seen him" (John 14:6–7).

These two sentences, which immediately follow the "I am the
way and the truth and the life" statement, essentially say that the
heart of God is found only by pursuing the *presence* of God. Jesus
made it clear that he is the I Am who reveals God. He is God's
presence. The truth is a person, and his name is Jesus.

You see, each group in Jesus' day told the "story of everything." The fundamental story that animated all groups in Judaism had the following elements: God is the Creator; this God is our God; there is but one God; this one God chose us to be a light to the world; this God formed a covenant with us through Abraham; this God, through Moses, gave us the Law to guide us in the ways of God; we sin against this Law and the temple sacrifices restore us to God; God sends prophets to reveal God's message to us; the prophets speak words about our sins, judgment, repentance, and promise; if we don't repent, our sins lead to captivity, exile, and suffering; we've discovered that revival and restoration occur when we turn back to God and the covenant. And each group in Judaism offered the best way to turn back to God's covenant.

Jesus fit into that story himself—until other groups thought he didn't fit. But he did.

The truth is, truth is not an easy game to play.

Deconstructors have grabbed on to this the way a mama lion grasps her baby in her massive jaws and teeth to move it to safety. They're in it for truth, not for simplicities and superficialities. Jon Ward, the *Yahoo! News* journalist we referred to in chapter 4, calls himself a "border-stalker" in his pursuit of truth—someone who wants to examine not just two sides but all sides. He wants to pursue and even find the truth. Take a moment to read and ponder what he wrote:

> I thought, naively, that this [pursuit of truth] was a straight-forward task. It never is. Dishonesty pays—and pays well. These have been especially hard years for the pursuit of truth. The modern world is a violent environment for a border-stalker. It is now the norm to be intolerant of opposing views,

to see others as *the other*: to fear them, to hate them. Black-and-white thinking is everywhere. Nuance is vanishing. Complexity is demonized. . . .

This is my account of trying to walk the path Jesus spoke of, despite all the ways I've seen the pursuit of truth sidelined, dismissed, and blocked, often in the name of faith. It has felt bleak at times. This has pushed me deeper into the most essential teachings of my childhood faith. . . .

From a young age, I latched on to the idea that truth is central to Christian faith. I've always loved the way that Jesus stood for truth. "I am the way and the truth and the life," Christ said (John 14:6). At another point, he promised that his Spirit would "guide you into all the truth" (16:13). When he was about to be executed, Jesus told a Roman official, "The reason I was born and came into the world is to testify to the truth" (18:37). "What is truth?" replied Pontius Pilate, the Roman governor (18:38). It's a haunting question. . . .

The process by which we find [truth] is maybe the most important thing. It takes work to locate, and often as soon as we think we have grasped it, it slips away. Truth is not a script. It is not a cheat sheet for life. Truth does not come from picking a set of answers and then arranging all the questions so that they line up correctly. Truth starts with the questions. It requires an openness—to other points of view and experiences, to being wrong, to changing one's mind. A commitment to truth involves a passionate embrace of critical thinking.[5]

Ward never labels himself a deconstructor. But he fits the profile of many today in how he pursues truth. It's not as certain or straightforward as it seemed in former years. It's a struggle. But the place to begin all over again is with Jesus. He is the Way, and the Way is a person on a path who calls others to follow him on the path.

Pixels Become Flesh

Several years ago, my wife and I (Tommy) were visiting my parents at their new home in upstate New York. We had a little extra cash and a few days away from the kids, so we took the train to New York City. We were invited by someone we got to know through Facebook and Instagram. She lived in Brooklyn with her husband, who was traveling for work, and she offered us a bedroom for the night.

When we finally met in real life, I was struck by how different she was from what I expected. Her voice was softer and more subdued than I imagined, her mannerisms more humble, and she was a little shorter than I expected. I had to make some adjustments as the old picture in my mind was replaced. The illusion of knowing someone from a distance was replaced with a truer knowledge of that person. The picture we had in our heads was like a mosaic of pieces, posts, images, and personality bits that were shining through. But then those pixels became flesh.

Our deconstructors camp out in that place as well. When Jesus says, "If you know me, you will know my Father as well" (John 14:7), he knows whereof he speaks. Jesus doesn't add *another* piece to the puzzle of God. He wipes mystery off the table and says, *Look at me, and you will know the Father.* Look at who Jesus spends his time with, look at how he sees people, look at how he responds to the pain and suffering in the world with compassion. When you see Jesus' character, you see the very character of God the Father. That's what Jesus says. For Jesus, the truth is a person—the pixels made flesh, as it were, God incarnate.

Philip, one of Jesus' disciples, overheard Jesus' teaching and replied, "Lord, show us the Father and that will be enough for us" (John 14:8). In this one sentence, Philip summed up the desires of all religions throughout human history: *Just tell me what God is like and what God wants. Give me the information.* Verses 9 and 10 capture Jesus' surprise at this request:

> Jesus answered: "Don't you know me, Philip, even after I have been among you such a long time? Anyone who has seen me has seen the Father. How can you say, 'Show us the Father'? Don't you believe that I am in the Father, and that the Father is in me?"

It's like Jesus says, *I know it's difficult. Something altogether new is now here. The true image stands before you. I am the truth!* Jesus is the Word made flesh (John 1:14). He is the complete message that God has for the world. When we think of God, the Father wants us to think of Jesus—the embodiment of human weakness and shame, with his beard ripped out and his nakedness exposed—every symbol of power and masculinity stripped from his body—and bearing the shame of the sinners on either side of him.

All of this is because God is not powerful in the same way we picture power (violent and coercive, strong and wealthy, with a good reputation and a rich pedigree). God is powerful in his display of weakness, in his fellowship with the broken, in his offer of forgiveness to sinners, and in the resurrection of the dead. Jesus is the truth.

A Dark Way

Not long after the disciples' conversation with Jesus in the upper room, everything unraveled. What happened to truth then? The disciples found themselves entering chaos and darkness. Their rabbi, Jesus, was arrested in the dark of night, tried, and unjustly executed. And as they gathered in the upper room in the days following Jesus' crucifixion, chaos swirled around them. Their faith and their lives became formless and void. Where was their hope? Where was their future? Could anything good come of this? Gone was any certainty.

What they did not grasp was that the Spirit of God was there, planting in the ground of that chaos the seeds of new life: Jesus' body—like a seed planted by the Spirit of God in the soil of the earth for three days, suddenly sprouting from the ground. At his resurrection, a new *imago Dei* was born—a *new* Adam, a *new* human, the *true* human. And all of this is just the beginning because Jesus is only the firstfruits of whoever follows him (1 Corinthians 15:23). Who*ever*.

Jesus still offers his bodily presence in today's world through his church. First in the Garden of Eden, then the temple in Jerusalem, then Jesus himself, and now the church is where heaven and earth come together, where God and humanity share space to be present with all those in the chaos, those in need of new life. When the church comes together as the body of Christ, the Spirit is present, planting new life and leading us on the path of truth to the Father. When the church eats the bread and drinks the wine, the church visibly speaks of the darkness that has become light.

Deconstructors understand what it is to look for the truth in the midst of chaos. They often feel there is no solid ground to stand on. They feel torn between their beliefs and their faith community. They have long thrown out any belief that their faith will grow. Many are dizzied by a slow slide taking them deeper into the hole of agnosticism. They are not where they once were, and they do not know where they are going. Yet they still wander in search of truth. Their experience is one of chaos, and as in Genesis 1, the Spirit is drawn to chaos. God meets us in the chaos for the same reason he met many of his prophets in the desert—it is the place where we learn how to live a life of faith.

We believe the Spirit is still working in the hearts of those who wander through the wilderness of deconstruction. The Spirit has every intention of creating a place for discovery, turning the swirl of chaos into the sweet order of the truth who is Jesus.

"The Way" in a Pluralistic Society

Many Bible verses have been used as instruments of division by people seeking power or struggling with fear. John 14:6 is one of those verses. Many who read Jesus' claim of being the Way—a phrase intended to set people free to walk the kingdom path to a life worth living—will gasp and say this type of speech is certaintist, intolerant, and dangerous. We live in a postmodern world that has witnessed the horrors of xenophobia, tribalism, and the religious oppression of the twentieth century. Nothing disturbs deconstructors today more than exclusivist claims to final, absolute truth in a world filled with complications and permutations.

Jesus was speaking to his own people in his people's way in his people's day. And that day was complicated by various groups advocating for their way of truth. But the context in which these words are read in today's world bring with it a different kind of complexity. We live in a pluralistic world shared by Jews, Christians, Hindus, Muslims, Buddhist monks, and proponents of millions of different worldviews all sharing the same physical space. There are questions we need to ask about what it looks like for Jesus to become Lord in the life of a Hindu or a Muslim.

Still, fruitful conversations about topics like this don't happen by speaking in hypotheticals. What matters most today is what mattered most in Jesus' world—*presence*. Jesus made the stunning claim that he was the very presence of God. In the flesh. Truth in a person remains the best witness. We are challenged to form relationships across cultural divides and to discern by God's Spirit how God is revealing Jesus as the way and the truth and the life.

Sometimes we use the words of Jesus to answer questions that weren't being asked in Jesus' day, and when we do this, things can get messy. Questions about who is right and who is wrong and weighing the merits of truth claims are all valid activities, especially considering the weight of what we are discussing. But misusing the words of Jesus is not the way to answer those questions, and an honest reading of the text will include reading it—as much as possible—in its original context.

Jesus' claim that he is the way, the truth, and the life is not outrageous or offensive. This claim was then and is today a reminder that God is near and is on a mission to bring *life* to our world. If Jesus is *the way*, then *all* can draw close to God. If Jesus is the way, the truth, and the life, deconstructors are right to ask, "Why do we not sit down with Jesus and listen to him?"

The Table of Jesus

The table was a tool of status and honor in the ancient world. Tables were the golf courses of the first century, the place where power brokers made their deals to increase and consolidate their power. Sitting at the table with those in power gave one access to the power, wealth, and influence they desired, so tables were the biggest of deals.

Jesus sets the table of honor and then announces, "So go to the street corners and invite to the banquet anyone you find" (Matthew 22:9). The "bad as well as the good" (22:10) came and sat at his table. Jesus shared his status with them, and he took their status on himself. He created a culture of humility and grace, where those at the bottom found comradery and fellowship in their lowliness as those at the top associated with the muck and the mire of society, those thrown out and rejected.

Jesus' table gatherings disrupted honor culture and replaced it with love culture. Jesus invited those from the margins of society—tax collectors, prostitutes, slaves, women, children, and everyone in between. He taught his followers not to judge those at the table with them, as is the pattern of the world. He didn't proclaim their sins, condemn them, or make sure they all agreed with position papers and doctrinal statements. Instead, he filled them up with whatever he had, whether tangible or spiritual.

The church is a *fellowship of differents*, a gathering of a diverse set of people with a bundle of differences and disagreements. The church is made up of cultural outsiders and insiders, and Christ's body brings them together as an alternative to the separations that world and empire demand. Together—every tribe and tongue, culture and color, nuance and politic. For the church to be absent of any single demographic is not an act of Jesus; it is an act of culture.

Jesus gathered both traditional Jews and progressive Romans; celibate apostles conversed with Ethiopian eunuchs (Acts 8:26–40), none of whom would fit the standards of the modern church. If any group is left outside, the church must know that Jesus will be found outside with them, gathering, feeding, and loving all those marginalized by the church.

This model of life is precisely why the early church chose the dinner table to symbolize the gathering of the followers of Jesus. It is why sharing a meal together was the central activity of the early church and why the Lord's Supper is still the center of most Christian gatherings today, because it means *everyone has access to what Jesus is offering.*

The Eyes of Jesus

Sometimes our eyes are *fixed*, and sometimes our eyes *rest* on something. It is the difference between an intense stare and a soft gaze. Perhaps it is easiest to say that we *fix* our eyes on the thing we *desire*; we *rest* our eyes on the things we *love*.

In generations past, those pursuing leadership were taught to fix their eyes on their goal the way people like Christopher Columbus did—with bravery and sacrifice. But these days, Columbus's diary has gained much unwanted attention, mainly for his description of the Native Americans he met when he arrived on this uncharted continent. He describes them as naïve and ignorant of evil, even while noting their immense generosity. And instead of praising their generosity, he wrote in his log, "I could conquer the whole of them with fifty men, and govern them as I pleased."[6]

Columbus has come under the ire of younger generations raised with access to information that wasn't available to their parents. For them, Columbus reflects the graspers and hirelings who look out on the crowds of people and see a market, whose eyes rest on themselves and who are fixed on the goal of influence and power over others.

Those who knew Jesus best said his eyes *rested* on the crowds before him. Matthew wrote, "When he saw the crowds, he had compassion on them, because they were harassed and helpless, like sheep without a shepherd" (Matthew 9:36). What a moving description! Harassed and helpless is his description for the masses of people with no one to follow. The people were searching for something good to eat, somewhere safe to sleep. They were being devoured by wolves, so they ran into the arms of a shepherd who abused them, lied to them, and used them for his own gain. Jesus' eyes fell on them with a soft gaze, and "he had compassion on them."

When the eyes of Jesus rest on people, he asks if they have direction, if they have had anything to eat. He wonders if they have a place to ask their questions and guidance to discern the path they should take. They are not just another untapped market to exploit in order to build a bigger kingdom. He doesn't first think, *We need to plant a church here*, but rather says, "The harvest is plentiful but the workers are few" (Matthew 9:37). In other words, *I'm going to need more shepherds.*

The masses of deconstructing Christians today are under the resting eye of Jesus. Yes, they wander. And sadly, they no longer trust their shepherds. They have been disillusioned, abused, and gaslighted. They are "harassed and helpless, like sheep without a shepherd." But as Jesus said, "The harvest is plentiful but the workers are few." So, following his direction, we "ask the Lord of the harvest, therefore, to send out workers into his harvest field" (Matthew 9:38). Our prayer is that by listening to deconstructors and the disillusioned—those who are asking questions and raising challenges—we can begin to inspire a new generation of good shepherds. We need shepherds whose eyes are *fixed* on Jesus and *rest* on his sheep.

The Hand of Jesus

In 2005, then-president George W. Bush traveled to Saudi Arabia to do some politicking. He wanted to bring down the price of oil, but he also wanted to show the world that four years after 9/11, Americans and the Saudis were not enemies. How did he do this? By holding hands and taking a walk with the Saudi prince. Americans pointed and giggled at this awkward display, but the Saudis saw that as a clear display of friendship and honor. They were flattered by the gesture because it symbolized their hopes for friendship and a shared future. Humans link hands to give or receive guidance, show affection, and communicate to those around them that there is a shared bond.

On the world stage today, whose hand is Jesus reaching out to hold? And as you think about that question, consider a closely related follow-up question: Whose hand is the evangelical church in America reaching out to hold? We hope these two questions have the same answer, but if they did, we probably wouldn't have written this book.

The Gospels present us with a Jesus who ignored the hands of those in power, the ones who would give him the greatest level of influence in this world. These are not the hands you and I typically think we ought to ignore, and if they ever reach out for us, we are quick to respond. Power, wealth, and influence make life easier. Holding hands with one of those "values" will likely bring the other two, and almost everyone believes they would be far better off in life if they possessed all three.

But the Gospels present us with a Jesus who is simply not interested in any of those worldly aims. Instead, he allows himself to become the ire of those who wield these gifts. Timothy

Gombis tells us that "when Jesus earned the title 'friend of sinners' (Matt. 11:19), it was not the sweet and tender title near to the heart of forgiven saints. It was a dismissive epithet applied to one who was an obstacle to the Pharisaic program of working to bring about resurrection."[7] Jesus held hands with sinners. On the public stage, no less. And it earned him the ire of the powerful around him.

In the eyes of the *religious* authorities, holding hands with people on the margins contaminated the people of God. That very act threatened the perception of holiness the religious institution demanded. And in the eyes of the *political* authorities, holding hands with people on the margins upset the culture of honor and status. It threatened the boundaries between the classes.

Jesus did this *on purpose*, and the gospel writers recorded his actions *on purpose* so the early church might have a clear picture of what the body of Christ should be doing in the world. Jesus didn't want the early church to reach for the hands of personal ease, but rather, like Jesus at the tomb, reach down to those in need of resurrection.

Those who have become deconstructors *for Christ's sake* have heard the Jesus call to disrupt the religious and political powers of our world by holding hands with those on the margins. The church has all too often responded by calling them friends of sinners—and they don't mean that as a compliment. Their presence, along with the presence of the unwanted people they have brought to church with them, has caused disruption. Church elders have plotted against them and schemed, through conversations in church parking lots and in late-night elder meetings, how to get rid of them.

To deconstructors looking for a conversation, it feels more

like a crucifixion. But this is, of course, how the power of God is released—on the cross. Many of today's deconstructors understand that God works through cross-shaped acts, and if holding hands with outsiders will win them the ire of the powerful, it just may be the most potent act of embodiment. It brings the story of Jesus into our world today. And so they hold the hands of those whom Jesus is reaching for.

If we must be disruptive, let's do it for Christ's sake.

Notes

Chapter 1: Encountering Jesus in Fundamentalism

1. Lydia Saad, "Military Brass, Judges among Professions at New Image Lows," Gallup, January 12, 2022, https://news.gallup.com/poll/388649/military-brass-judges-among-professions-new-image-lows.aspx; see also Aaron Earls, "Pastors and Churches Face Historic Lack of Trust," LifeWay Research, July 12, 2022, https://research.lifeway.com/2022/07/12/pastors-and-churches-face-historic-lack-of-trust.

2. Earls, "Historic Lack of Trust."

3. Bob Smietana, *Reorganized Religion: The Reshaping of the American Church and Why It Matters* (New York: Worthy, 2022).

4. The term *Nones* describes people who define themselves as atheistic, agnostic, or "nothing in particular" with regard to religious affiliation. The term *Dones* (also known as *Nonverts*) describes people who have put religious commitment in their past. For more on Nonverts, see Stephen Bullivant, *The Nonverts: The Making of Ex-Christian America* (New York: Oxford University Press, 2022). Our concern here is not so much with Nonverts as it is with deconstructors. While we're listening to Nonverts, we are in discussion with deconstructors.

5. This question is the title of a 1972 Larry Norman song.

6. Gene Raskin, "Those Were the Days," Mary Hopkin, performer, 1968, single.

7. Todd Hunter, *What Jesus Intended: Finding True Faith in the Rubble of Bad Religion* (Downers Grove, IL: InterVarsity, 2023), 9.

Chapter 2: Hearing from Jesus in Our Doubts

1. Cited in HC proprietary research, 2022 U.S. General Book Study among nationally representative U.S. book buyers/readers aged 18+who have considered changing their beliefs.
2. HC proprietary research; see also Marissa Postell Sullivan, "Churchgoers Less Familiar Than Pastors with Deconstruction, More Likely to See It in Their Pews," Lifeway Research, July 25, 2023, https://research.lifeway.com/2023/07/25/churchgoers-less -familiar-than-pastors-with-deconstruction-more-likely-to-see-it -in-their-pews.
3. Josh Packard and Casper ter Kuile, "Gen Z Is Keeping the Faith. Just Don't Expect to See Them at Worship," Religion News Service, September 23, 2021, https://religionnews.com/2021/09 /23/gen-z-is-keeping-the-faith-just-dont-expect-to-see-them-at -worship.
4. Olivia Jackson, *(Un)Certain: A Collective Memoir of Deconstructing Faith* (London: SCM, 2023), 73.
5. Rohadi Nagassar, *When We Belong: Reclaiming Christianity on the Margins* (Windsor, Ontario: Herald, 2022), 24.
6. HC proprietary research.
7. Ryan P. Burge, *20 Myths about Religion and Politics in America* (Minneapolis: Fortress, 2022).
8. Quoted in Tish Harrison Warren, "The State of Evangelical America," *New York Times*, July 30, 2023, www.nytimes.com /2023/07/30/opinion/state-of-evangelical-america.html.
9. Tony Keddie, *Republican Jesus: How the Right Has Rewritten the Gospels* (Berkeley: University of California Press, 2020).
10. Martyn Wendell Jones, "Jesus and the Enemy-Making Machine," *Wheaton* 23, no. 1 (Winter 2020), https://magazine.wheaton.edu /stories/winter-2020-feature-enemy-making-machine; David

Fitch, *The Church of Us vs. Them: Freedom from a Faith That Feeds on Making Enemies* (Grand Rapids, Brazos, 2019).

11. Sara Billups, *Orphaned Believers: How a Generation of Christian Exiles Can Find the Way Home* (Grand Rapids: Baker, 2022), 14.
12. Jesse T. Jackson, "Matt Chandler Responds to Deconstruction Controversy," Church Leaders, December 8, 2021, https://churchleaders.com/news/412237-matt-chandler-responds-to-deconstruction-controversy.html.
13. A. J. Swoboda, *After Doubt: How to Question Your Faith without Losing It* (Grand Rapids: Brazos, 2021), 6.
14. David F. Ford, *The Gospel of John: A Theological Commentary* (Grand Rapids: Baker Academic, 2021), 273.
15. Swoboda, *After Doubt*, 41.
16. Quoted in Jackson, *(Un)Certain*, 209.

Chapter 3: Interlude: Three Phases of Deconstruction

1. See Jim Davis and Michael Graham, *The Great Dechurching: Who's Leaving, Why Are They Going, and What Will It Take to Bring Them back?* (Grand Rapids: Zondervan, 2023), 49, 61, 75, 90–91, 107–8.
2. We appreciate A. J. Swoboda's sketch of the three stages of faith development: construction, deconstruction, reconstruction (*After Doubt: How to Question Your Faith without Losing It* [Grand Rapids: Brazos, 2021], 23–28). In this book, however, it can feel patronizing to inform a deconstructor that she is merely in the second stage and that the third stage, like Easter, is coming. So buck up, good days are ahead.
3. Steven Curtis Chapman, "Blind Lead the Blind," track 6 on *For the Sake of the Call*, December 1990.
4. Geoff Moore & The Distance, "Evolution . . . Redefined," track 1 on *Evolution*, 1993.
5. Dan Kimball, *They Like Jesus but Not the Church* (Grand Rapids: Zondervan, 2007).

6. Meghan Larissa Good, *Divine Gravity: Sparking a Movement to Recover a Better Christian Story* (Harrisonburg, VA: Herald, 2023).

7. What follows is based on the wonderful essay by Paul G. Hiebert titled "Conversion, Culture and Cognitive Categories," *Gospel in Context* 1, no. 4 (1978): 24–29, https://danutm.files.wordpress .com/2010/06/hiebert-paul-g-conversion-culture-and-cognitive -categories.pdf.

8. There are various ways of clarifying the orders of important beliefs from the center out or from the foundation up: Jesus, Bible, creed, confessions, statements of faith, theological systems, and so forth. Scot discusses an approach like this in his book *Five Things Biblical Scholars Wish Theologians Knew* (Downers Grove, IL: IVP Academic, 2021).

Chapter 4: Losing Jesus in Our Politics

1. Quotations in this section are taken from Jon Ward, *Testimony: Inside the Evangelical Movement That Failed a Generation* (Grand Rapids: Brazos, 2023), 197, 206, 230, 237.

2. Bob Smietana, *Reorganized Religion: The Reshaping of the American Church and Why It Matters* (New York: Worthy, 2022), 39.

3. John 6:9.

4. John 6:20 CEB.

5. Exodus 3:14 (CEB).

6. Richard Bauckham, *The Testimony of the Beloved Disciple* (Grand Rapids: Baker Academic, 2007), 245–47.

7. Isaiah 43:10–11, 13; 45:3.

8. Ryan P. Burge, *The Nones: Where They Came From, Who They Are, and Where They Are Going* (Minneapolis: Fortress, 2021), 53, 70.

9. Tony Keddie, *Republican Jesus: How the Right Has Rewritten the Gospels* (Oakland: University of California Press, 2020), 1–2.

10. Keddie, *Republican Jesus*, 75.

11. Among other titles, Bill O'Reilly and Martin Dugard's *Killing Jesus: A History* serves as a good example for Keddie.

12. Ben Folds Five, "Away When You Were Here," track 9 on *The Sound of the Life of the Mind* (Sony Music Entertainment, 2012).

13. Personal communication. Used with permission.

Chapter 5: Placing Jesus in the Center

1. Katie Gaddini, *The Struggle to Stay: Why Single Evangelical Women Are Leaving the Church* (New York: Columbia University Press, 2022), xiii. Quotations that follow in the next few paragraphs are from pages 158, 168, 216, 218–19.

2. Mary Daly, *Beyond God the Father: Toward a Philosophy of Women's Liberation* (Boston: Beacon, 1973), 19.

3. See Joshua Bote, "He Wrote the Christian Case against Dating. Now He's Splitting from His Wife and Faith," *USA Today*, July 29, 2019, https://amp.usatoday.com/amp/1857934001.

4. John 6:68–69. The stories in the previous paragraphs can be found in John 6.

5. Lee Strobel, *The Case for Faith: A Journalist Investigates the Toughest Objections to Christianity*, updated and expanded ed. (Grand Rapids: Zondervan, 2021), 13–14.

6. John 12:21.

7. Cited in Jeffrey M. Jones, "U.S. Church Membership Falls Below Majority for First Time," Gallup, March 29, 2021, https://news.gallup.com/poll/341963/church-membership-falls-below-majority-first-time.aspx.

8. Ryan P. Burge, "Mainline Protestants Are Still Declining, but That's Not Good News for Evangelicals," *Christianity Today*, July 13, 2021, www.christianitytoday.com/news/2021/july/mainline-protestant-evangelical-decline-survey-us-nones.html.

9. Burge, "Mainline Protestants," italics added.

10. Burge, "Mainline Protestants."

11. Ryan Burge, "What Does Denominational Decline Look Like," Graphs about Religion, May 9, 2023, www.graphsaboutreligion.com/p/what-does-denominational-decline, italics added.

12. Olivia Jackson, *(Un)Certain: A Collective Memoir of Deconstructing Faith* (London: SCM, 2023), 50, italics added.

13. Jackson, *(Un)Certain*, 149.

14. Scot McKnight, *The Second Testament: A New Translation* (Downers Grove, IL: InterVarsity, 2023).

Chapter 6: Interlude: Deconstruction Is Conversion

1. Lewis R. Rambo, *Understanding Religious Conversion* (New Haven, CT: Yale University Press, 1995. I (Scot) applied his theory to conversion in the Gospels in *Turning to Jesus: The Sociology of Conversion in the Gospels* (Louisville: Westminster John Knox, 2002).

Chapter 7: Burying Jesus in Production

1. Olivia Jackson, *(Un)Certain: A Collective Memoir of Deconstructing Faith* (London: SCM, 2023), xiv, xvi. It seems the majority of the subjects in her study did not reconstruct as we describe it in our book. She prefers *integration* instead and describes a much wider experience that refers more to finding oneself, wherever that may be. Another good example of integration is Shannon Harris, *The Woman They Wanted: Shattering the Illusion of the Good Christian Life* (Minneapolis: Broadleaf, 2023).

2. Martin Luther, "A Mighty Fortress Is Our God" (1529). Public domain.

3. Bob Smietana, "How Bethel and Hillsong Took Over Our Worship Sets," *Christianity Today*, April 12, 2023, www.christianitytoday.com/news/2023/april/bethel-hillsong-worship-sound-christian-research.html.

4. Smietana, "How Bethel and Hillsong."

5. See N. T. Wright, *Matthew for Everyone, Part 2: Chapters 16-28* (Louisville, KY: Westminster John Knox, 2004), 13–15.

6. See Jim Davis and Michael Graham, *The Great Dechurching: Who's Leaving, Why Are They Going, and What Will It Take to Bring Them Back?* (Grand Rapids: Zondervan, 2023), 39–96, 122–25.

7. Sean McDowell and John Marriott, *Set Adrift: Deconstructing What You Believe without Sinking Your Faith* (Grand Rapids: Zondervan, 2023), xi–xii.

8. "World Hunger Facts: What You Need to Know in 2023," Concern Worldwide, October 12, 2023, https://concernusa.org/news/world-hunger-facts.

9. Matthew 14:13–21; Mark 6:30–44; Luke 9:10–17; John 6:1–15.

10. Cited in Robert Smietana, *Reorganized Religion: The Reshaping of the American Church and Why It Matters* (New York: Worthy, 2022), 45.

11. The quotes in this paragraph are from Miroslav Volf and Ryan McAnnally-Linz, *The Home of God: A Brief Story of Everything* (Grand Rapids: Brazos, 2022), 131. A flourishing of ordinary life in the beauty of God has been the heart of Volf's work for the past decade. See also Miroslav Volf, *A Public Faith: How Followers of Christ Should Serve the Common Good* (Grand Rapids: Brazos, 2011); Miroslav Volf, *Flourishing: Why We Need Religion in a Globalized World* (Yale University Press, 2016); Miroslav Volf and Matthew Croasmun, *For the Life of the World: Theology That Makes a Difference* (Grand Rapids: Brazos, 2019).

12. C. S. Lewis, *The Weight of Glory, and Other Addresses* (San Francisco: HarperSanFrancisco, 1980), 140, italics added.

Chapter 8: Joining Jesus in the Light

1. For a recent woman's story of growing up in the tradition of a woman's role as childbearing and homemaking, along with her examination of 1 Timothy 2 in light of the Artemis cult, see Sandra L. Glahn, *Nobody's Mother: Artemis of the Ephesians in Antiquity and the New Testament* (Downers Grove, IL: IVP Academic, 2023). For another, see Cait West, *Rift: A Memoir of Breaking Away from Christian Patriarchy* (Grand Rapids: Eerdmans, 2024).

2. Leonardo Blair, "Dove-Award Winning Gungor Rattles Christian World with Revelation That They Don't Believe the Bible

Literally," *Christian Post*, August 5, 2014, www.christianpost.com
/news/dove-award-winning-gungor-rattles-christian-world-with
-revelation-that-they-dont-believe-the-bible-literally-124373.
3. Wendell Berry, *Jayber Crow: A Novel*, Port William 6 (Berkeley,
CA: Counterpoint, 2000), 53–54.
4. Michelle Knight, Threads post, August 14, 2023, www.threads
.net/@michelleknight/post/Cv7xc1KOtpR.
5. Berry, *Jayber Crow*, 54.

Chapter 9: Seeing Jesus at the Door

1. Ralph Ellison, *Invisible Man*, 2nd ed. (New York: Random House,
1952; New York: Vintage, 1995), 3–4. Citations refer to the
Vintage edition. Italics appear in the Vintage edition text.
2. Robert Smietana, *Reorganized Religion: The Reshaping of the
American Church and Why It Matters* (New York: Worthy, 2022),
9, 14.
3. See Jim Davis and Michael Graham, *The Great Dechurching: Who's
Leaving, Why Are They Going, and What Will It Take to Bring Them
Back?* (Grand Rapids: Zondervan, 2023), A culture Christian is
someone who doesn't distinguish American from Christian or
Southern from Christian, or, for that matter, Irish from Catholic
or Swedish from Lutheran.
4. P. D. James, *Death in Holy Orders*, reissue ed. (Toronto: Knopf,
2001; New York: Ballantine, 2007), 174. Citation refers to the
Ballantine edition.

Chapter 10: Encountering Jesus in the Shepherd

1. Sean McDowell and John Marriott, *Set Adrift: Deconstructing
What You Believe without Sinking Your Faith* (Grand Rapids:
Zondervan, 2023), xv–xvi.
2. Quoted in Olivia Jackson, *(Un)Certain: A Collective Memoir of
Deconstructing Faith* (London: SCM, 2023), 33.
3. Phyllis Tickle, *The Great Emergence: How Christianity Is Changing
and Why* (Grand Rapids: Baker, 2008), 19.

4. Tickle, *Great Emergence*, 21.

5. Lisa Oakley, "Understanding Spiritual Abuse," *Church Times*, February 16, 2018, www.churchtimes.co.uk/articles/2018/16 -february/comment/opinion/understanding-spiritual-abuse.

6. For a good study of spiritual abuse rooted in Ezekiel, see Amy White, *Towards a Theological Definition of Spiritual Abuse: Ezekiel 34 and the Use of Pastoral Power* (Nottingham: Grove, 2021).

7. Cited in Peter Preskar, "The Roman Emperor—the Most Dangerous Occupation in Ancient Rome," Short History, May 22, 2021, https://short-history.com/roman-emperor-9c4f67f5d36e.

8. Dallas Willard, *Living in Christ's Presence: Final Words on Heaven and the Kingdom of God* (Downers Grove, IL: InterVarsity, 2014), 17.

Chapter 11: Trusting Jesus at the Apocalypse

1. Quoted in Scot McKnight and Hauna Ondrey, *Finding Faith, Losing Faith: Stories of Conversion and Apostasy* (Waco, TX: Baylor University Press, 2008), 33–37.

2. See Fr. Jeremy, "Christ's Descent into Hades—Icon Explanation," Orthodox Road, December 2, 2012, www.orthodoxroad.com /christs-descent-into-hell-icon-explanation.

3. "User Clip: Rep. Justin Pearson Closing Remarks," C-Span, April 7, 2023, www.c-span.org/video/?c5065450/user-clip-rep-justin -pearson-closing-remarks (transcribed by Scot).

4. See HC proprietary research, 2022 U.S. General Book Study among nationally representative U.S. book buyers/readers aged 18+ who have considered changing their beliefs.

5. There were no Gallup or Pew polls in the first century.

6. Timothy G. Gombis, *Power in Weakness: Paul's Transformed Vision for Ministry* (Grand Rapids: Eerdmans, 2021), 93.

Chapter 12: Discerning Jesus as the Way

1. Adam Hamilton, *Seeing Gray in a World of Black and White: Thoughts on Religion, Morality, and Politics* (Nashville: Abingdon, 2012).

2. A philosophical discussion of certainty, often thought to be a knowledge claim about something that is indubitable, can be found here: https://plato.stanford.edu/entries/certainty. We are using the term *certainty* in the sense of a cocksure claim about religious claims believed knowable and known (God exists, Jesus was raised, the creation story fits science).

3. Robert Chao Romero and Jeff M. Liou, *Christianity and Critical Race Theory: A Faithful and Constructive Conversation* (Grand Rapids: Baker Academic, 2023), 105.

4. Christopher Troeger, "Just How Do Deaths Due to COVID-19 Stack Up?," Think Global Health, February 15, 2023, www .thinkglobalhealth.org/article/just-how-do-deaths-due-covid-19 -stack. About the number of people who lost their lives because of COVID-19, Troeger writes, "These tallies could substantially underestimate COVID-19's true death toll. In fact, some estimates suggest the total number of deaths could be more than two times as large as reported globally—nearly eighteen million deaths—and more than ten times greater than reported in some countries."

5. Jon Ward, *Testimony: Inside the Evangelical Movement That Failed a Generation* (Grand Rapids: Brazos, 2023), 4–6.

6. "Excerpts from Christopher Columbus' Log, 1492 A.D.," Franciscan Archives, www.franciscan-archive.org/columbus /opera/excerpts.html.

7. Timothy G. Gombis, *Power in Weakness: Paul's Transformed Vision for Ministry* (Grand Rapids: Eerdmans, 2021), 54.